INSPIRATIONS™
Baby

country bumpkin

COUNTRY BUMPKIN
PUBLICATIONS

Your children are not your children.

They are the sons and daughters of Life's longing for itself.

They come through you but not from you,

And though they are with you yet they belong not to you.

You may give them your love but not your thoughts,

For they have their own thoughts.

You may house their bodies but not their souls,

For their souls dwell in the house of tomorrow,

Which you cannot visit, not even in your dreams.

from THE PROPHET - KAHILL GIBRAN

CONTENTS

STEP-BY-STEP STITCH INSTRUCTIONS

11 *Smocker's knot*   17 *Granitos*   45 *Eyelets*   49 *Loop stitch*
52 *Shadow work variation*   53 *Twirled ribbon rose*   67 *Grab stitch*
74 *Pleating*   75 *Trellis stitch*   82 *Raised stem stitch*

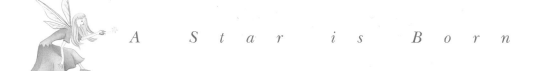
THE
Receiving Shawl

by KRIS RICHARDS *of* SOUTH AUSTRALIA

When I inhaled I breathed in peaches dangling on sylvan boughs.

When she suckled I understood the smile on the face of the Madonna.

And so we embarked on our endless honeymoon, our lovely first years.

JILL NEVILLE, CUTTING THE CORD

Receiving Shawl

*W*rap *your new arrival in the soft comfort of an embroidered welcoming shawl*

made of ivory winter twill. The flowing lettering on the top corner is accented

with roses and daisies while on the reverse side a simplified spray and filigree design

is repeated on the remaining corners.

——— *The finished shawl measures 85cm (33 ½") square* ———

REQUIREMENTS

Fabric
*2.4m x 112cm wide (2yd 22 ½" x 44")
ivory winter twill*

Threads & Needles
See page 8.

Supplies
*3.2m (3yd 18") cream satin
mini piping*

*77cm (30 ¼") square of non-fusible
thin wadding (eg. Pellon)*

Water-soluble fabric marker

CUTTING OUT

*See the centre liftout pattern for the
cutting layout.*

Cut two pieces of winter twill, each
77cm (30 ¼") square for the shawl.

Cut six strips of winter twill, each
12cm x 112cm wide (4 ¾" x 44") for
the frill.

PREPARATION FOR EMBROIDERY

*See the centre liftout pattern for the
embroidery designs.*

Using a black pen, trace the embroidery designs, including all placement
lines, onto tracing paper.

Front
Tape the main embroidery design to
a window or light box. With the right
side facing you, place one square of
fabric over the design, aligning the
raw edges with the placement lines.
The light shining through will make
the design visible through the fabric.

Using the water-soluble fabric
marker, lightly trace the outlines of
the lettering. Mark the centre of the
circles for the roses, rosebuds and
daisies with a small dot. Lightly mark
the outlines and centre veins of the
large leaves and the positions for the
stems of the fronds. Trace over the
curved outline for the corner.
Transfer the curve to the three
remaining corners of the fabric.

Back
On the remaining square of fabric,
transfer the single spray and filigree
design to three corners in the same
manner as the main embroidery
design. Transfer the curve to all four
corners of the back, as before.

Spread the thin wadding out flat.
With the right side uppermost, place
the back fabric over the wadding. Pin
and tack the back and wadding
together in a grid pattern *(diag 1)*.
Treat the back and wadding as
one layer when embroidering and
assembling the blanket.

Diag 1
Tacking

Main embroidery design

Filigree design

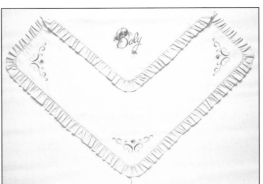

I love these little people, and it is not a slight thing when they, who are so fresh from God, love us.

— DICKENS —

MBROIDERY

See page 11 for step-by-step instruction for working a smocker's knot.

A delicate cluster of bullion roses and buds decorates the beautiful lettering on the top corner of the shawl. On the reverse side, a single spray surrounded by stem stitch filigree, is positioned on the remaining three corners.

Use the no. 7 straw needle when working the bullion knots and the no. 9 crewel needle for all other embroidery.

Order of Work

Main Design

Embroider the letters first, stitching them in the order in which you would write. Using stem stitch, outline all the letters including the areas which will be covered with the flowers and leaves. Fill in the outlines with stem stitch, adding extra rows to cover the wider areas of the letters.

Stitch the large fly stitch leaves, beginning each one at the tip and adding a smocker's knot to the base.

Work the bullion roses and buds, starting each one at the marked centre and working outwards. Add a calyx to each rosebud by working a detached chain on each side of the outer petals. Add a third detached chain at the centre. Work the stems to the rosebuds in stem stitch. Using the same thread, stitch detached chain leaves near the base of the rosebud stems on all stems except those positioned on the 'Y'.

Changing thread colour, embroider pairs of detached chain leaves beside the roses. Nestle French knot buds around the roses, placing them singly or in clusters of two or three. Embroider the daisies using detached chain and place a French knot at each centre.

Finally work the stems of the pale green fronds. Add the detached chain leaves, using a long anchoring stitch for each one.

Filigree designs

Outline the filigree designs with stem stitch and then fill the shapes, adding extra rows in the wider areas as before.

Work the fly stitch leaves, followed by the single bullion rose. Add the scattered French knots, detached chain leaves, partial daisies and then the fronds.

CONSTRUCTION

See the centre liftout pattern.

THREADS & NEEDLES

DMC stranded cotton

A = 223 lt shell pink
B = 224 vy lt shell pink
C = 225 ultra lt shell pink
D = 640 vy dk beige-grey
E = 677 vy lt old gold
F = 834 vy lt golden olive
G = 3012 med khaki green
H = 3024 vy lt Jacobean green
I = 3743 vy lt antique violet

Madeira stranded cotton

J = 0901 lt blue-violet (2 skeins)

No. 7 straw (milliner's) needle
No. 9 crewel embroidery needle

THESE DESIGNS USE

*Bullion knot, Detached chain,
Fly stitch, French knot,
Smocker's knot, Stem stitch*

EMBROIDERY KEY

All embroidery is worked with two strands of thread unless otherwise specified.

Lettering

Outline = J (1 strand, stem stitch)
Filling = J (1 strand, stem stitch)

Filigree

Outline = J (1 strand, stem stitch)
Filling = J (1 strand, stem stitch)

Large leaves = D (fly stitch, smocker's knot)

Roses

Centre = A
(1 - 2 bullion knots, 8 wraps)

Inner petals = B (3 bullion knots, 12 - 15 wraps)

Outer petals = C (3 - 7 bullion knots, 15 wraps)

Rosebuds

Centre = B
(1 - 2 bullion knots, 10 wraps)

Outer petals = C (2 - 4 bullion knots, 10 wraps)

Calyx = D (1 strand, detached chain)

Stem = D (1 strand, stem stitch)

Leaves = D (1 strand, detached chain) or none

Small leaves = G (detached chain)

Golden buds = E or F (French knot, 2 wraps)

Daisies

Petals = I (1 strand, detached chain)

Centre = I (1 strand, French knot, 2 wraps)

Fronds

Stems = H (1 strand, stem stitch)

Leaves = H (1 strand, detached chain)

One hot summer morning a little Cloud rose out of the sea and floated lightly and happily across the blue sky. Far below lay the Earth, brown, dry, and desolate, from drought. The little Cloud could see the poor people of the Earth working and suffering in the hot fields, while she herself floated on the morning breeze, hither and thither, without a care.

"Oh, if I could only help the poor people down there!" she thought. "If I could but make their work easier, or give the hungry ones food, or the thirsty a drink!"

And as the day passed, and the Cloud became larger, this wish to do something for the people of Earth was ever greater in her heart.

On Earth it grew hotter and hotter; the sun burned down so fiercely that the people were fainting in its rays; it seemed as if they must die of heat, and yet they were obliged to go on with their work, for they were very poor. Sometimes they stood and looked up at the Cloud, as if they were praying, and saying, "Ah, if you could help us!"

"I will help you; I will!" said the Cloud. And she began to sink softly down toward the Earth. But suddenly, as she floated down, she remembered something which had been told to her when she was a tiny Cloud-child, in the lap of Mother Ocean; it had been whispered that if the Clouds go too near the Earth they die. When she remembered this she held herself from sinking, and swayed here

and there on the breeze, thinking - thinking. But at last she stood quite still, and spoke boldly and proudly. She said "Men of Earth, I will help you, come what may!"

The thought made her suddenly, marvellously, big and strong and powerful. Never had she dreamed that she could be so big. Like a mighty angel of blessing she stood above the Earth, and lifted her head and spread her wings far over the fields and woods. She was so great, so majestic, that men and animals were awe-struck at the sight; the trees and the grasses bowed before her; yet all the earth-creatures felt that she meant them well.

"Yes, I will help you," cried the Cloud once more. "Take me to yourselves; I will give my life for you!"

As she said the words a wonderful light glowed from her heart, the sound of thunder rolled through the sky, and a love greater than words can tell filled the Cloud; down, down, close to the Earth she swept, and gave up her life in a blessed, healing shower of rain.

That rain was the Cloud's great deed; it was her death, too; but it was also her glory. Over the whole country-side, as far as the rain fell a lovely rainbow sprang its arch, and all the brightest rays of heaven made its colours; it was the last greeting of a love so great that it sacrificed itself.

Soon that, too, was gone, but long, long afterward the men and animals who were saved by the Cloud kept her blessing in their hearts.

I was just a little thing, When a fairy came and kissed me;

Floating in upon the light, Of a haunted summer night.

WRAPPING THE BABY

1. First fold. With the back uppermost, fold down the top corner diagonally to show the main embroidery design.

2. Holding the folded corner in place, turn the shawl over. Lay the baby on the shawl.

3. Second fold. Diagonally fold in one side corner.

4. Third fold. Diagonally fold up the lower corner.

5. Fourth fold. Diagonally fold in the remaining side.

6. Back view.

16th century

ADVICE TO MOTHERS

BY SIMON DE VALLAMBERT

"Send babies to sleep by rocking them, singing to them softly, placing them near running water, if possible, by making water fall drop by drop into a basin, avoiding all noise, giving them fresh scents to smell.

To bring on sleep, place some oil of violet or rose in his nose with lettuce juice, adding a drop of oil of anise, and put on top of the head oil of poppy or waterlily, sometimes adding a grain of opium."

S M O C K E R ' S   K N O T

A smocker's knot is much firmer than a French knot. It is often used as a secure technique for finishing off a thread on the back of the fabric in smocking and other embroidery but it can also be used as a decorative stitch. For the step-by-step photographs we used no. 3 perlé cotton.

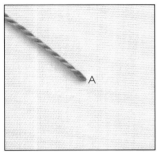

1. Bring the thread to the front at A.

2. Keeping the thread above the needle, take a tiny back stitch from B to A.

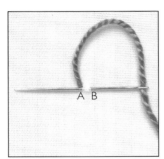

3. Pull the thread through, leaving a small loop approximately 1cm (³⁄₈") long.

4. Take the needle through the loop.

5. Pull the thread through, leaving a second loop approximately 1cm (³⁄₈") long.

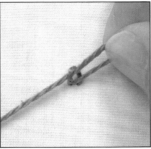

6. Holding the thread in the left hand and the second loop in the right hand, begin to pull the second loop.

7. Pull until the first loop is tight against the fabric. The second loop remains intact.

8. Take the needle through the second loop.

9. Begin to pull the thread through.

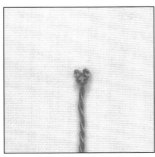

10. Pull the thread until a firm knot forms against the fabric.

11. Take the needle to the back of the fabric under the knot.

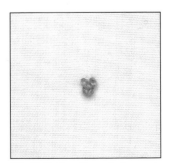

12. Pull the thread through and end off on the back. **Completed smocker's knot.**

FOR THE
Nursery

by Jenny Saladine of Western Australia

Door Swag

O̶ur earliest memories of childhood are often those of our nursery.
Create a little haven on earth with this embroidered damask door swag –
a lovely and practical means of keeping the nursery door ajar whilst baby sleeps.

If making both the door swag and nappy pincushion 25cm x 112cm wide (9 ¾" x 44") of both the damask and homespun is required.

REQUIREMENTS

Fabric
20cm x 60cm wide (8" x 23 ⅝") piece of ivory cotton damask
20cm x 60cm wide (8" x 23 ⅝") piece of ivory lightweight homespun

Threads & Needles
See page 18.

Supplies
65cm (25 ½") ivory piping
Small amount of polyester fibre-fill
1.6m x 4mm wide (1yd 27" x ³⁄₁₆") ivory cotton ribbon
10cm (4") embroidery hoop
20cm x 30cm wide (8" x 11 ¾") piece of wax free transfer paper (eg. Saral)

PREPARATION FOR EMBROIDERY
See the centre liftout pattern for the embroidery designs and pattern.

Cutting out
Cut one piece of ivory cotton damask and one piece of homespun, each 20cm x 30cm wide (8" x 11 ¾").

Transferring the designs and pattern
Trace the pattern piece, including the embroidery designs, onto lightweight interfacing and transfer all pattern markings.

Lay the piece of damask, right side up, on a flat surface. Place the transfer paper onto the damask with the colour side down. Centre the tracing, design side up, over the transfer paper. Ensure there is enough fabric beyond the embroidery designs to enable the use of a hoop.

Using a ball point pen and pressing firmly, trace the outlines for the bears with a fine line and mark the positions for their eyes and noses with dots. Mark the flower heads with small dots and indicate the stems of the hollyhocks with curved lines. Transfer the pattern markings and remove the tracing and transfer paper. Do not cut out the piece until after the embroidery is worked.

Preparing the fabric
Lay the piece of homespun out flat. Position the damask, right side up, over the homespun. Tack the two layers together approximately 1.5cm (⅝") inside the marked cutting line. Treat them as one layer from now on.

EMBROIDERY
See page 17 for step-by-step instructions for granitos.

Use the chenille needle for stitching the wool bears. The straw needle is used for working the bullion knots and the crewel needle is used for all other embroidery. Place the fabric in the hoop when embroidering the bears, the granitos and the French knots.

Diag 1

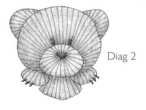

Diag 2

Whoever teaches his son

teaches not only his son

but also his son's son –

and so on to the end

of generations.

TALMUD

A babe in a house is a well-spring of pleasure, a messenger of peace and love,

a resting-place for innocence on earth, a link between angels and men.

~ TUPPER ~

· · · · · · · The finished door swag measures 8cm x 22cm wide (3 ⅛" x 8 ⅝") · · · · · · ·

Order of work

Sitting bear

Work the eyes and nose using the chocolate coloured stranded cotton. For each eye, stitch two horizontal straight stitches and cover these with two vertical straight stitches. Fill the triangular shape of the nose with horizontal straight stitches.

Change to the chenille needle and the crewel wool. Referring to the diagram for the direction of the satin stitches, stitch the bear. Starting at the middle of the bear's head, fill the left hand side with satin stitches, fanning them around the shape of the head. Take the wool under the stitches on the back of the fabric and emerge at the middle. Fill the right hand side of the bear's head in the same manner. Work the outer ears in satin stitch, beginning at the middle as before. Stitch the body and arms and then work the paws, placing the satin stitches so they surround the space for the paw pads. Change the yarn colour and work the muzzle, radiating the stitches from the nose outwards. Fill the inner ears and paw pads. Add the claws with straight stitches using the chocolate stranded cotton (diag 1).

Peeping bear

Following the diagram for the direction of satin stitches, embroider the second bear, peeping from the bed of flowers, in a similar manner to the sitting bear (diag 2).

Pink roses

A group of bullion roses is placed on each side of both bears. Stitch the centre of each rose with two bullion knots. Surround these with three bullion knot petals.

For the larger roses, add a second round of petals consisting of two bullion knots. Work one to two bullion knots for the petals of the rosebuds.

Embroider a bullion knot leaf on each side of the roses. Add the stems and lower leaves with straight stitches and add straight stitches to the tops of the roses. Stitch the leaves and stems of the rosebuds using straight stitch.

Hollyhocks

Four spires of hollyhocks, two pearl grey and two baby blue, are placed behind the sitting bear. Two smaller spires, one pearl grey and one baby blue, are positioned on the right hand side of the peeping bear.

Stitch the four-petalled flowers first, forming each petal with a granitos.

Add a golden brown French knot at the centre of each flower.

Work a single granitos for the bud at the top of each spire. Embroider the stem and leaves for the bud in fly stitch and work the stem and upper leaves for the flowers using straight stitch. Add detached chain leaves at the base of the pearl grey hollyhocks.

Lavender

A spray of lavender grows near the side of the head of both bears and a smaller spray above the roses on the right hand side of the peeping bear.

Embroider the stems and leaves with straight and fly stitches. Add bullion knot flowers at the tips.

Forget-me-nots

Stitch the flowers at the base of the peeping bear in the same manner as the hollyhock flowers. Add the leaves in straight stitch.

Pale gold flowers

Embroider straight stitches for the stems and leaves at the top of the peeping bear and below the forget-me-nots. Scatter old gold French knots randomly among the stems.

CONSTRUCTION

See the centre liftout pattern.

Pin Cushion

This embroidered and piped nappy pincushion has two seated bears surrounded by a colourful cottage garden. The finished pincushion measures 16.5cm (6 ¹/₂") square.

REQUIREMENTS

Fabric

22cm x 50cm wide (8 ⁵/₈" x 19 ⁵/₈") piece of ivory cotton damask

22cm x 50cm wide (8 ⁵/₈" x 19 ⁵/₈") piece of ivory lightweight homespun

Threads & Needles

See page 19.

Supplies

75cm (29 ¹/₂") ivory piping

Small amount of polyester fibre-fill

2 x 17mm (⁹/₁₆") wide covered buttons

10cm (4") embroidery hoop

22cm (8 ⁵/₈") square of wax free transfer paper (eg. Saral)

Water-soluble fabric marker

PREPARATION FOR EMBROIDERY

See the centre liftout pattern for the embroidery design and pattern.

Cutting out

Cut one piece of cotton damask and one piece of homespun, each 22cm (8 ⁵/₈") square.

Transferring the design

Trace the pattern piece, including the embroidery design and all pattern markings, onto lightweight interfacing.

Lay the piece of damask, right side up, on a flat surface. Place the transfer paper onto the damask with the colour side down. Aligning the top right hand corner of the pattern with the top right hand corner of the damask, place the interfacing, design side up, over the transfer paper. Ensure there is enough fabric beyond the embroidery design on the lower left hand corner to enable the use of a hoop.

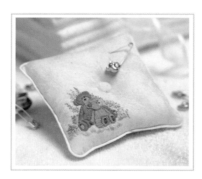

Using a ball point pen and pressing firmly, transfer the design in the same manner as the door swag. Do not cut out the piece until after the embroidery is worked.

Preparing the fabric

Lay the piece of homespun out flat. Position the marked damask, right side up, over the homespun. Tack the two layers together approximately 1.5cm (⁵/₈") inside the marked cutting line. Treat these as a single layer from now on.

EMBROIDERY

See page 17 for step-by-step instructions for granitos.

Use the chenille needle for stitching the wool bears. The straw needle is used for working the bullion knots and the crewel needle is used for all other embroidery. Place the fabric in the hoop when embroidering the bears, the granitos and the French knots.

As the embroidery is stitched in the same manner as the door swag, refer to the previous instructions for working each element of the design.

Order of work

Bears

Refer to the diagram for the direction of the satin stitching on both bears *(diag 3)*. Work the large bear first, followed by the smaller bear.

Pink roses

A group of roses is placed on each side of the bears.

Hollyhocks

Two baby blue and two pearl grey spires of hollyhocks are placed behind the larger bear.

Lavender

A spray of lavender is positioned on each side of the design.

Forget-me-nots

Four flowers are stitched on the right hand side, below the roses.

Grass

Embroider the patches of grass at the base of the design with straight stitch, slightly varying the length and angle of the stitches.

CONSTRUCTION

See the centre liftout pattern.

Diag 3

THESE DESIGNS USE

Detached chain, Fly stitch,

French knot, Granitos,

Satin stitch, Straight stitch,

Bullion knot

GRANITOS

Also known as rondels, granitos are quick and easy to do. The number of straight stitches used in each one can vary depending on the size and plumpness of the stitch you wish to achieve. For the step-by-step photographs we used three strands of stranded cotton.

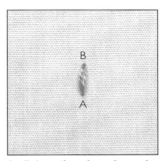

1. Bring the thread to the front at A and take it to the back at B. Pull the thread through to form a straight stitch.

2. Bring the needle to the front at A again, taking care to emerge through exactly the same hole in the fabric.

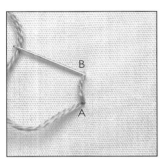

3. Pull the thread through. Take the needle to the back at B through exactly the same hole in the fabric as the first straight stitch.

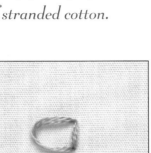

4. Loop the thread to the left hand side of the first stitch and begin to gently pull the thread through.

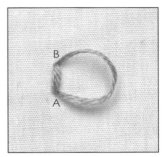

5. Pull until the stitch lies alongside the first stitch. Re-emerge at A again and take the thread to the back at B. Loop the thread to the right and gently pull it through.

6. Continue working stitches, alternating from side to side, until the granitos is the desired plumpness. **Completed granitos.**

CONTENTMENT *by* EUGENE FIELD

Once on a time an old red hen
Went strutting round with
pompous clucks,
For she had little babies ten,
A part of which were tiny ducks.
"Tis very rare that hens," said she,
"Have baby ducks as well as chicks –
But I possess, as you can see,
Of chickens four and ducklings six!"

A season later, this old hen
Appeared, still cackling of her luck,
For, though she boasted babies ten,
Not one among them was a duck!
"Tis well," she murmured,
brooding o'er
The little chicks of fleecy down,
"My babies now will stay ashore,
And, consequently, cannot drown!"

The following spring the old red hen
Clucked just as proudly as of yore –
But lo! her babes were ducklings ten,
Instead of chickens as before!
"Tis better," said the old red hen,
As she surveyed her waddling brood;
"A little water now and then
Will surely do my darlings good!"

But, oh! alas, how very sad!
When gentle spring rolled
round again,
The eggs eventuated bad,
And childless was the old red hen!
Yet patiently she bore her woe,
And still she wore a cheerful air,
And said; "Tis best these things
are so,
For babies are a dreadful care!"

I half suspect that many men,
And many, many women, too,
Could learn a lesson from the hen
With foliage of vermilion hue.
She ne'er presumed to take offence
At any fate that might befall,
But meekly bowed to Providence –
She was contented – that was all!

THREADS & NEEDLES

Appletons 2 ply crewel wool

A = 691 ultra lt honeysuckle yellow

B = 882 cream

C = 901 vy lt golden brown

D = 981 ultra lt putty groundings

DMC stranded cotton

E = 223 lt shell pink

F = 224 vy lt shell pink

G = 225 ultra lt shell pink

H = 415 pearl grey

I = 524 vy lt fern green

J = 644 med beige-grey

K = 677 vy lt old gold

L = 775 baby blue

M = 838 dk chocolate

N = 3042 lt antique violet

O = 3053 green-grey

P = 3827 vy lt golden brown

No. 9 crewel embroidery needle

No. 9 straw (milliner's) needle

No. 22 chenille needle

EMBROIDERY KEY

All embroidery is worked with one strand of thread unless otherwise specified.

Sitting bear

Eyes = M (straight stitch)

Nose = M (straight stitch)

Head = C (satin stitch)

Outer ear = C (satin stitch)

Body = C (satin stitch)

Arms = C (satin stitch)

Outer paws = C (satin stitch)

Inner ear = A (satin stitch)

Muzzle = A (satin stitch)

Paw pads = A (satin stitch)

Claws = M (straight stitch)

Peeping bear

Eyes = M (straight stitch)

Nose = M (straight stitch)

Head = D (satin stitch)

Ears = D (satin stitch)

Upper body = D (satin stitch)

Paws = D (satin stitch)

Muzzle = B (satin stitch)

Claws = M (straight stitch)

Pink roses

Centre = E or F
(2 bullion knots, 6 wraps)

Inner petals = F or G
(3 bullion knots, 9 wraps)

Outer petals = G (2 bullion knots, 11 wraps) or none

Leaves = O (1 bullion knot, 6 wraps, straight stitch)

Stems = O (straight stitch)

Rosebuds

Buds = F (1 - 2 bullion knots, 6 wraps)

Calyx = I (fly stitch, 2 bullion knots, 9 wraps)

Leaves = I (straight stitch)

Stems = I (straight stitch)

Hollyhocks

Petals = H or L (granitos)

Centre = P (French knot, 1 wrap)

Stems and leaves = O (straight stitch, detached chain)

Bud = H or L (granitos)

Bud stem and leaves = O (fly stitch)

Lavender

Flowers = N (bullion knot, 7 wraps)

Stem and leaves = I and J (fly stitch, straight stitch)

Forget-me-nots

Petals = L (granitos)

Centre = P (French knot, 1 wrap)

Leaves = O (straight stitch)

Pale gold flowers

Flowers = K (French knot, 1 - 2 wraps)

Stems = I or J (straight stitch)

BABY NAMES *related to* FLOWERS

Alfalfa	Camelina	Dahlia	Orchid
Althaea	Camellia	Daisy	Peony
Amaryllis	Carnation	Daphne	Petunia
Angelica	Chervil	Erica	Rose
Anise	Cicely	Heather	Rosemary
Aster	Cinnamon	Ivy	Sage
Azalea	Clover	Jasmine	Silene
Basil	Coriander	Lilac	Tulip
Bellis	Cosmos	Lily	Veronica
Burnet	Cypress	Marigold	Violet
Buttercup	Daffodil	Mariposa	Willow

THREADS & NEEDLES

Appletons 2 ply crewel wool

A = 691 *ultra lt honeysuckle yellow*

B = 882 *cream*

C = 901 *vy lt golden brown*

D = 981 *ultra lt putty groundings*

E = 986 *dk putty groundings*

DMC stranded cotton

F = 223 *lt shell pink*

G = 224 *vy lt shell pink*

H = 225 *ultra lt shell pink*

I = 415 *pearl grey*

J = 524 *vy lt fern green*

K = 775 *baby blue*

L = 838 *dk chocolate*

M = 3042 *lt antique violet*

N = 3052 *med green-grey*

O = 3053 *green-grey*

P = 3827 *vy lt golden brown*

No. 9 crewel embroidery needle

No. 9 straw (milliner's) needle

No. 22 chenille needle

EMBROIDERY KEY

All embroidery is worked with one strand of thread unless otherwise specified.

Large bear

Eyes = L (straight stitch)

Nose = L (straight stitch)

Head = C (satin stitch)

Ears = C (satin stitch)

Body = C (satin stitch)

Arms and legs = C (satin stitch)

Paws = C (satin stitch)

Muzzle = A (satin stitch)

Paw pad = A (satin stitch)

Claws = L (straight stitch)

Small bear

Eyes = L (straight stitch)

Nose = L (straight stitch)

Head = D (satin stitch)

Outer ears = D (satin stitch)

Body = D (satin stitch)

Arms and legs = D (satin stitch)

Paws = D (satin stitch)

Muzzle = B (satin stitch)

Inner ear = E (satin stitch)

Paw pads = E (satin stitch)

Claws = L (straight stitch)

Pink roses

Centre = F or G (2 bullion knots, 6 wraps)

Inner petals = G or H (2 - 3 bullion knots, 9 wraps)

Outer petals = H (2 bullion knots, 11 wraps) or none

Leaves = N or O (1 bullion knot, 6 wraps, straight stitch)

Stems = J or O (straight stitch)

Rosebuds

Buds = G or H (1 - 2 bullion knots, 6 wraps)

Calyx = J (fly stitch)

Leaves = J (straight stitch)

Stems = J (straight stitch)

Hollyhocks

Petals = I or K (granitos)

Centre = P (French knot, 1 wrap)

Stems and leaves = N (straight stitch, detached chain)

Bud = I or K (granitos)

Bud stem and leaves = N (fly stitch)

Lavender

Flowers = M (bullion knot, 7 wraps)

Stem and leaves = J (fly stitch, straight stitch)

Forget-me-nots

Petals = K (granitos)

Centre = P (French knot, 1 wrap)

Stems = O (straight stitch)

Leaves = N (detached chain, straight stitch)

Grass = J (straight stitch)

BABY NAMES *related to* VIRTUES

Charity	Hope
Chastity	Hospitality
Compassion	Joy
Constance	Justice
Courtesy	Kindness
Faith	Knowledge
Gentle	Love
Goodness	Patience
Harmony	Peace
Holiness	Purity
Honesty	Truth
Honor	Wisdom

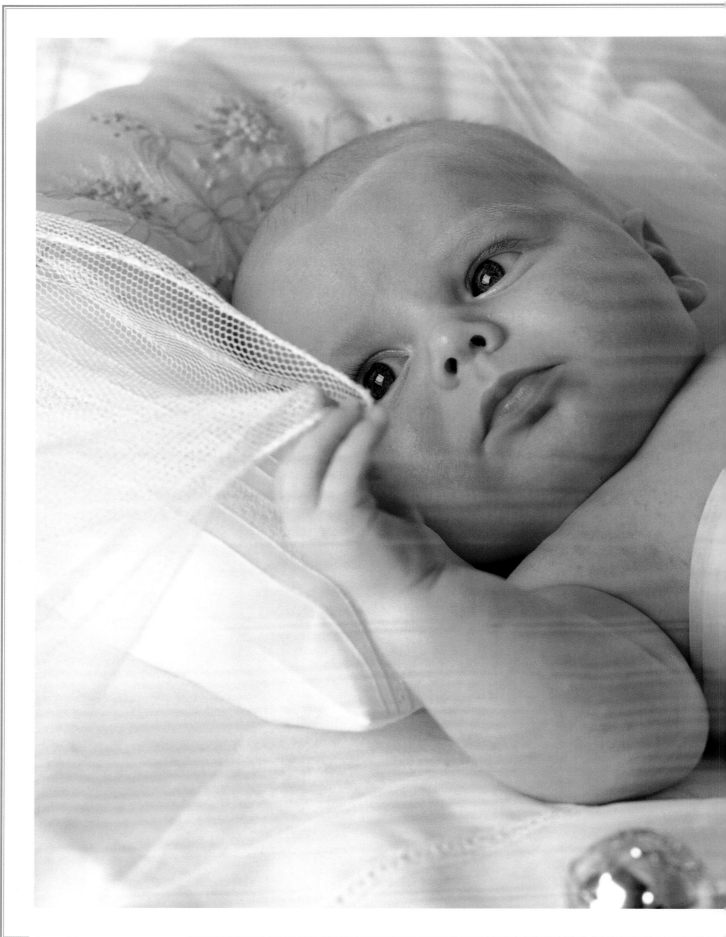

THE
Bed Linen

by ALLA AKSELROD *of* VICTORIA

Bed Linen

Only the finest voile, the most exquisite embroidery and the softest lace
are good enough to wrap around your precious infant.

Fabric & Lace

1.3m x 112cm wide (1yd 15" x 44")
white cotton voile

3.1m x 12mm wide (3yd 14" x ½")
white cotton lace insertion

Threads & Needles

See page 25.

Supplies

Mettler #60/2 white heirloom
sewing thread

15cm (6") embroidery hoop

0.5 mechanical lead pencil

CUTTING OUT

Square the piece of voile by pulling a thread along one cut edge and carefully cutting along the pulled thread line.

Sheet

Measure 91.5cm (36") down the length and pull a thread across the fabric. Cut along the pulled thread line.

Pull a thread along one side of the sheet beside the selvedge. Measure 110.5cm (43 ½") across from this line and pull a thread down the second side at this measurement. Cut along both pulled thread lines.

Pillowslip

Pulling threads in the same manner, cut a piece of fabric 30.5cm x 93cm wide (12" x 36 ⅝").

PREPARATION FOR EMBROIDERY

See the centre liftout pattern for the embroidery designs.

Sheet

Marking the placement for the centre motif
Fold the fabric in half down the length. At the top edge, measure down the fold for 17cm (6 ¾") and mark with a pin. Open the fabric out flat with the right side facing and with the marked pin at the top end of the sheet.

To the left of the centre, measure across 8cm (3 ³/₁₆") and mark with a pin. Measure down 16.8cm (6 ⅝") from the top raw edge and mark with a pin. Using the lead pencil, mark the position where the two measurements meet (*see diag 1*).

Again from the centre point, measure across to the right 8.8cm (3 ½") and mark with a pin. Measure down 17.3cm (6 ⅞") from the top raw edge. Mark as before at the position where the two measurements meet. These points are the positions for the outermost blue spots nestling near the ends of the trailing tendrils (*diag 1*).

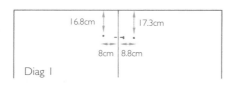

Diag 1

Marking the placements
for the line of rosebuds and spots
On the left of the design, measure across 40cm (15 ¾") from the centre and mark with a pin. Measure down 16.8cm (6 ⅝") from the top edge and mark with a pin. Mark the point where the measurements meet.

Keeping the measurement the same from the top edge, and working from the marked point towards the centre, mark six more points, spacing each 4.5cm (1 ¾") apart. Using the same measurements, repeat the procedure on the right hand side (*diag 2*).

Diag 2

Transferring the design
With the right side of the fabric facing you, place the top of the sheet over the embroidery design. Ensure the marks on the fabric are aligned with the corresponding spots on the design. Pin in place to prevent movement.

Using the lead pencil, trace the outlines of the bow, ties and trailing tendrils. Mark the positions of the flowers, buds and spots with small dots.

Pillowslip

Marking the placement for the design
From the top left hand side of the fabric, measure across 39cm (15 ⅜") on one long side and mark with a pin. This is the position for the fold line between the front and back. From the pin, measure across a further 37.8cm (14 ⅞") and mark with a pin. There will be 16.2cm (6 ⅜") remaining for the turnback. Repeat on the opposite long side, measuring from the lower left hand side. Fold and press the fabric at the marked positions. Unfold the fabric (*diag 3*).

Diag 3

The finished sheet measures 102.5cm x 89cm wide (40 ³⁄₈" x 35")
and the finished pillowslip measures 28.5cm x 36cm wide (11 ¹⁄₄" x 14 ¹⁄₈")

Pillowslip embroidery

Sheet embroidery

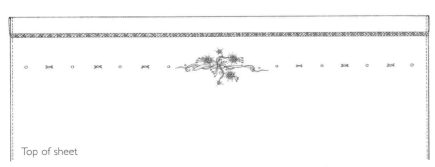

Top of sheet

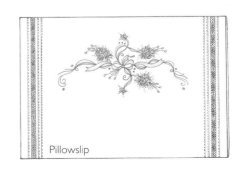

Pillowslip

From the first fold line, measure across 9.5cm (3 ¾") to the right. Measure down 13.5cm (5 ⅜") from the top raw edge. Using the lead pencil, mark the position where the two measurements meet.

From the turnback fold line, measure across 9cm (3 ½") to the left and measure down 13.5cm (5 ⅜") from the top raw edge. Mark the position where the two measurements meet.

These marks are the positions for the blue spots below the ends of the trailing tendrils *(diag 4).*

Diag 4		
	13.5cm	
	13.5cm	
9.5cm		9cm

Transferring the design

With the right side of the fabric facing you, place the top of the pillowslip over the embroidery design in the centre liftout pattern. Ensure the marks on the fabric are aligned with the corresponding spots on the design. Pin in place to prevent movement.

Using the lead pencil, trace the outlines of the bow, ties and trailing tendrils. Mark the positions of the flowers, buds and spots with small dots.

EMBROIDERY

See page 17 for step-by-step instructions for granitos and page 52 for the shadow work variation.

A gently flowing bow, embroidered with a variation of shadow work, is centred amid delicate bouquets on the sheet turnback. Lustrous padded satin stitch buds fall softly from the side of each bouquet. A single trailing rose and a cluster of padded

satin stitch buds reach out above and below the centre of the bow. A row of alternating spots and tiny rosebuds extend from the design to the sides of the sheet. The pillowslip features a similar central motif.

Use the straw needle for the bullion knots and the crewel needle for all other embroidery. Place the fabric in the hoop for all embroidery except the bullion knots and stem stitching.

Order of Work

Bow
Beginning at the bow knot, outline the bow and ties in back stitch. To work the shadow embroidery, turn the fabric over to the wrong side. Stitch from side to side within the shape to be filled. Take the needle and thread through the back of the outline stitches, taking care not to go through the fabric.

Bouquets
Embroider the large four-petalled flowers first. For each flower, stitch one petal followed by the opposite petal, rather than stitching around the flower. Stitch the remaining pair of petals and add the satin stitch centre.

Work the side view roses, starting with the centre bullion and working outwards. Position two of the outer petals at the base of the rose. Embroider two bullion knots side by side for the small blue rosebuds and a granitos for each tiny green bud. Work the white trailing buds in padded satin stitch. Stitch the stems and leaves and surround the bouquets with seed stitch and French knot specks. Add long straight stitches among the stems of the trailing buds.

Trailing roses
Work the bullion side view roses in the same manner as those in the bouquets. Add straight stitch leaves and then seed stitch and French knot specks around the rose. Stitch the stems in stem stitch, working the light blue stem first. Where the darker blue and white lines meet the previous row, take them behind the first row.

Buds and tendrils
Work the white trailing buds on each side of the bow knot in padded satin stitch. Embroider the stems and tendrils in stem stitch. Add long straight stitches between the stems.

Blue spots
Add the blue spots with granitos, nestling them around the bow and among the trailing tendrils.

Scattered spots and rosebuds on sheet
Finally, for the sheet, work the padded satin stitch spots alternating them with bullion rosebuds. Stitch two bullion knots for the petals of the rosebuds and add small straight stitches at each end for the leaves.

CONSTRUCTION

See the centre liftout pattern.

THESE DESIGNS USE

*Back stitch, Bullion knot,
French knot, Granitos, Seed stitch,
Padded satin stitch,
Shadow work variation, Satin stitch,
Stem stitch, Straight stitch*

THREADS & NEEDLES

DMC stranded cotton

A = *blanc*

B = *524 vy lt fern green*

C = *644 med beige-grey*

D = *745 vy lt yellow*

E = *3752 vy lt antique blue*

F = *3753 ultra lt antique blue*

G = *3756 lt baby blue*

DMC stranded rayon

H = *35200 snow white*

No. 8 straw (milliner's) needle

No. 9 crewel embroidery needle

EMBROIDERY KEY

All embroidery is worked with one strand of thread unless otherwise specified.

Bow

Outline = F (back stitch)

Filling = E (shadow work)

Bouquets
Four-petalled flowers
Petals = H (granitos)

Centre = D (satin stitch)

Side view roses

Centre = E (2 strands, bullion knot, 6 wraps)

Inner petals = G (2 strands, 2 bullion knots, 6 - 8 wraps)

Outer petals = A (2 strands, 4 bullion knots, 9 - 14 wraps)

Stamens = B (straight stitch)

Blue rosebuds

Petals = E (2 strands, 2 bullion knots, 9 wraps)

Stamens = B (straight stitch)

Green buds = B (granitos)

Stems = B or C (stem stitch)

Leaves = B or C (straight stitch)

Specks = A (seed stitch, French knot, 1 wrap)

Trailing roses

Side view rose

Centre = G (2 strands, 2 bullion knots, 9 wraps)

Outer petals = A (2 strands, 4 bullion knots, 9 - 14 wraps)

Stamens = B (straight stitch)

Leaves = B or C (straight stitch)

Tendrils = F, G or H (stem stitch)

Specks = A (seed stitch, French knot, 1 wrap)

Buds and tendrils

Buds = G (padding), H (satin stitch)

Stems = G (stem stitch)

Stem highlights = H (straight stitch)

Tendrils = F, G or H (stem stitch)

Blue spots = E (2 strands, granitos)

Scattered spots and rosebuds on sheet

Rosebuds

Petals = F (2 strands, 2 bullion knots, 10 wraps)

Leaves = B (straight stitch)

Spots = G (padding), H (satin stitch)

WHAT IS THE LITTLE ONE THINKING ABOUT?
VERY WONDERFUL THINGS, NO DOUBT;
UNWRITTEN HISTORY! UNFATHOMED MYSTERY!
YET HE LAUGHS AND CRIES, AND EATS AND DRINKS,
AND CHUCKLES AND CROWS, AND NODS AND WINKS,
AS IF HIS HEAD WERE AS FULL OF KINKS,
AND CURIOUS RIDDLES AS ANY SPHINX!

J G HOLLAND

ESSENTIAL UNDERGARMENTS BY JENNY BROWN & GABRIELLE FRANCIS
BOTH OF SOUTH AUSTRALIA

The Cow Jumped Over the Moon

BY JENNY BROWN

REQUIREMENTS

White 100% cotton singlet or vest with lace trim

Threads & Needles
See page 29.

Supplies
10cm x 14cm wide (4" x 5 ½") piece of wax free transfer paper (eg. Saral)

10cm x 14cm wide (4" x 5 ½") piece of heavy non-woven interfacing

10cm x 14cm wide (4" x 5 ½") piece of cardboard

PREPARATION FOR EMBROIDERY

See the centre liftout pattern for the embroidery design.

Preparing the singlet
With the back of the shoulders and armholes right sides together, fold the singlet down the length of the garment. Mark the centre front fold with a pin at the neckline and again 9cm (3 ½") down from the top edge of the lace at the neck.

Transferring the embroidery design
Open the singlet out flat with the front uppermost. Place the piece of cardboard between the front and back chest area.

Trace the design and placement lines onto the piece of interfacing.

Place the piece of transfer paper, with the colour side down, onto the chest area of the singlet front. Place the interfacing, design side up, over the transfer paper. Ensure the placement lines on the design match the neckline and pins in the singlet. Using a ball point pen and pressing firmly, trace the outline of the moon, the cow, its markings, and the lines for the shooting star trails. Mark the position of each star with a dot.

EMBROIDERY

Use the straw needle for working the bullion knots and the crewel needle for all other embroidery.

"As the knit fabric

is designed to allow

for stretch, do not pull the

stitches too tightly."

JENNY

Order of Work
Cow
Work the outline for the body, legs and tail with back stitch, keeping the stitches the same length as the rib in the knit fabric.

Stitch tightly clustered French knots for the markings on the body. Using the same colour thread, embroider the ears with detached chains and the eye with tiny straight stitches. For the tail tip, work two tapered bullion knots side by side.

Using the pink thread, work the udder with two horizontal bullion knots placed side by side. Use nine wraps for the top bullion knot and fourteen wraps for the knot beneath.

Stitch three tiny fly stitches for the teats. Embroider the nose with two tiny straight stitches.

Work the horns with two fly stitches in the yellow thread.

Shooting stars and trails
Using the ribs in the knit as a guide for stitch length and working on one side of the design, stitch the central row of the trail with running stitch. Begin near the position for the stars and end off the thread near the cow's hoof. Stitch two more rows on each side of the central line. Repeat for the shooting star trails on the opposite side.

Stitch the group of stars at the end of one trail. Embroider a small cross stitch for each star. Loosely carry the thread behind the fabric between the stars. Work the second group of stars in the same manner.

Stitch stars around each armhole, running the thread loosely within the seam allowance on the inside between each star. Space each star approximately 8mm (5/16") apart.

Moon
Embroider three yellow bullion knots for the moon. Work thirty wraps for the upper bullion knot, forty wraps for the middle knot and twenty three wraps for the lower knot. Curve each bullion to shape and couch in place with one strand of matching thread. Stitch two fly stitches for the nose, placing one inside the other.

Change to the beige thread and work a French knot for the eye and two back stitches for the mouth.

Many people have said to me "What a pity you had such a big family to raise. Think of the novels and the short stories and the poems you never had time to write because of that." And I looked at my children and I said, "These are my poems. These are my short stories." OLGA MASTERS

EMBROIDERY KEY *for the* COW JUMPED OVER THE MOON

THREADS & NEEDLES

DMC stranded cotton

A = 310 black

B = 744 lt yellow

C = 761 lt salmon

D = 841 lt beige

E = 842 vy lt beige

Anchor stranded cotton

F = 129 lt delft blue

No. 8 straw (milliner's) needle

No. 8 crewel embroidery needle

EMBROIDERY KEY

All embroidery is worked with one strand of thread unless otherwise specified.

Cow

Outline = E (2 strands, back stitch)

Tail = E (2 strands, back stitch)

Markings = A (French knot, 3 wraps)

Eye = A (straight stitch)

Ears = A (detached chain)

Tail tip = A (2 bullion knots, 9 wraps)

Udder = C (2 bullion knots, 9 and 14 wraps)

Teats = C (fly stitch)

Nose = C (straight stitch)

Horns = B (fly stitch)

Shooting stars and trails

Trails = F (running stitch)

Stars = B (cross stitch)

Moon = B (2 strands, 3 bullion knots, 23 - 40 wraps; 1 strand, couching)

Nose = B (fly stitch)

Eye = D (French knot, 2 wraps)

Mouth = D (back stitch)

THIS DESIGN USES

Back stitch, Bullion knot, Couching, Cross stitch, Detached chain, Fly stitch, French knot, Running stitch, Straight stitch

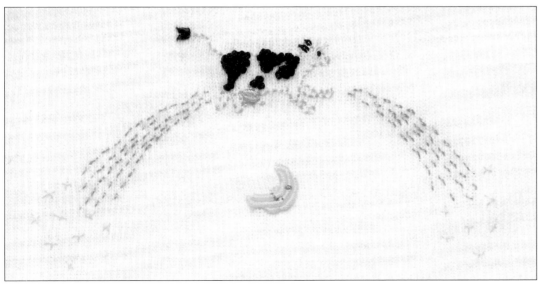

The finished embroidery design measures 5.5cm x 10cm wide (2 ¼" x 4")

The Bunny

BY GABRIELLE FRANCIS

REQUIREMENTS

White 100% cotton singlet or vest with lace trim

Threads & Needles

See page 31.

Supplies

8cm x 10cm wide (3 1/8" x 4") piece of wax free transfer paper (eg. Saral)

8cm x 10cm wide (3 1/8" x 4") piece of heavy non-woven interfacing

8cm x 10cm wide (3 1/8" x 4") piece of cardboard

PREPARATION FOR EMBROIDERY

See the centre liftout pattern for the embroidery design.

Preparing the singlet

With the back of the shoulders and armholes right sides together, fold the singlet down the length of the garment. Mark the centre front fold with a pin at the neckline and again 8.5cm (3 3/8") from the top edge of the lace at the neck.

Transferring the embroidery design

Open the singlet out flat with the front uppermost. Place the piece of cardboard between the front and back chest area.

Trace the embroidery design and placement lines onto the piece of heavy interfacing. Place the piece of transfer paper, with the colour side down, onto the chest area of the singlet front. Place the interfacing, design side up, over the transfer paper. Ensure the placement marks on the tracing match the pins on the singlet. Using a ball point pen and pressing firmly, trace the outline of the bunny. Mark the centre of the flowers with small dots and the positions for the stems and leaves with small lines.

EMBROIDERY

Use the no. 10 crewel needle when stitching with one strand of thread and the no. 8 crewel needle when stitching with three strands of thread.

Order of Work

Bunny

Work the ears with long vertical satin stitches. Begin at the centre and shape the ears by decreasing the length of the stitches as you progress to the sides. Fill the head with horizontal satin stitches.

Using the blue thread, embroider the jacket body with vertical stitches and the sleeves with diagonal stitches.

At the base of the jacket, stitch horizontal satin stitches for the hindquarters of the rabbit, decreasing the length towards the lower edge. Work the feet with diagonal satin stitches. Using the white thread, work three vertical stitches over the lower edge for the tail. Plump up the tail by passing the needle behind the stitches and gently pulling them into shape.

Add three straight stitches on each side of the head for the whiskers, making the centre stitch slightly longer than those on the outside.

Daisies

Work five or six detached chains for the petals of each daisy and add a yellow French knot for the centre. Embroider the stems in straight stitch and add two detached chains at the base for leaves.

Spots around armholes

Embroider blue French knots at approximately 2cm (3/4") intervals around each armhole. Between the spots, carry the thread loosely within the seam allowance on the inside.

THIS DESIGN USES

*Detached chain, French knot,
Satin stitch, Straight stitch*

THE SUN AND THE WIND

The Sun and the Wind once had a quarrel as to which was the stronger. Each believed himself to be the more powerful. While they were arguing they saw a traveller walking along the country highway, wearing a great cloak.

"Here is a chance to test our strength," said the Wind; "let us see which of us is strong enough to make that traveller take off his cloak; the one who can do that shall be acknowledged the more powerful."

"Agreed," said the Sun. Instantly the Wind began to blow; he puffed and tugged at the man's cloak, and raised a storm of hail and rain, to beat at it. But the cooler it grew and the more it stormed, the tighter the traveller held his cloak around him. The Wind could not get it off.

Now it was the Sun's turn. He shone with all his beams on the man's shoulders. As it grew hotter and hotter, the man unfastened his cloak; then he threw it back; at last he took it off! The Sun had won.

from STORIES TO TELL TO CHILDREN *by* SARA CONE BRYANT

EMBROIDERY KEY *for* THE BUNNY

THREADS & NEEDLES

DMC stranded cotton

A = *blanc*

B = *310 black*

C = *352 lt coral*

D = *368 lt pistachio green*

E = *648 lt beaver grey*

F = *727 lt golden yellow*

G = *932 lt antique blue*

No. 8 crewel embroidery needle

No. 10 crewel embroidery needle

EMBROIDERY KEY

All embroidery is worked with one strand of thread unless otherwise specified.

Bunny

Ears = E (satin stitch)

Head = E (satin stitch)

Jacket = G (satin stitch)

Hindquarters = E (satin stitch)

Tail = A (3 strands, satin stitch)

Whiskers = B (straight stitch)

Daisies

Petals = C (detached chain)

Centre = F (French knot, 1 wrap)

Stems = D (straight stitch)

Leaves = D (detached chain)

Spots = G (2 strands, French knot, 2 wraps)

The finished

embroidery design measures

2cm x 6.5cm wide

(¾" x 2 ⅝")

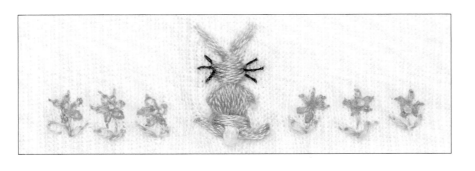

Play Time

BY JENNY BROWN

BY JENNY BROWN

REQUIREMENTS

White 100% cotton short sleeve body suit with binding trim

Threads & Needles
See page 35.

Supplies
8cm x 16cm wide (3 ⅛" x 6 ⅜") piece of wax free transfer paper (eg. Saral)

8cm x 16cm wide (3 ⅛" x 6 ⅜") piece of heavy non-woven interfacing

8cm x 16cm wide (3 ⅛" x 6 ⅜") piece of cardboard

PREPARATION FOR EMBROIDERY

See the centre liftout pattern for the embroidery design.

Preparing the body suit
With the back of the shoulders, sleeves and side seams right sides together, fold the body suit down the length of the garment. Mark the centre front fold with a pin at the neckline and again 8cm (3 ⅛") from the top edge of the binding at the neck.

Transferring the embroidery design
Open the body suit out flat with the front uppermost. Place the piece of cardboard between the front and back chest area.

Trace the embroidery design and placement lines onto the piece of heavy interfacing. Place the piece of transfer paper, colour side down, onto the chest area of the body suit front. Place the interfacing, design side up, over the transfer paper. Ensure the neck binding position and the placement lines on the design match the neckline and the pins on the body suit. Using a ball point pen and pressing firmly, trace the outline of the children. Use dots to mark the position of the ball, the spray of flowers and the three balloons.

EMBROIDERY

Use the straw needle for working the bullion knots and the crewel needle for all other embroidery.

"When stitching the clothes, I found it difficult to keep the sets of bullion knots together on the stretch fabric. After they were couched in the normal way, I ran a thread through the bullion knots from side to side. This pulled them together and kept them in the correct position." JENNY

Order of Work
Children
Work the body and clothes of the children in the same order, referring to the diagrams for the number of wraps used for the bullion knots. Begin with the clothing, couching the bullion knots in place and then pulling the knots together with a separate thread. Embroider the head, arms and legs next. For the child holding the balloons, taper the bullion knots at the ankles and add separate bullion knots for the feet. Stitch a French knot at the end of each arm for the hands. Work shoes on the first four children with bullion knots. Using straight stitches, embroider the hair of the girl with the flowers and the boy doing a handstand. For the remainder of the children, work the hair with French knots. Add straight stitches for eyes.

Ball
Work a bullion loop for the centre of the ball. Surround this with a second bullion loop and couch both in place. Stitch straight stitches over the base of the bullion loops.

Flowers
Work the stems, starting at the base of the flowers and extending past the hand. Collect the stems into a group and couch to the end of the hand. Stitch four French knots using the dusky pink thread and scatter four lavender French knots among them.

Balloons
Embroider the three strings using back stitch. Stitch the three balloons in the same manner as the ball, omitting the straight stitches at the base.

THIS DESIGN USES

Back stitch, Bullion knot, Bullion loop, Couching, French knot, Straight stitch

THREADS & NEEDLES

DMC stranded cotton
A = 211 lt lavender
B = 745 vy lt yellow
C = 760 salmon
D = 772 vy lt yellow-green
E = 799 med delft
F = 828 ultra lt blue
G = 840 med beige
H = 948 vy lt peach
I = 3828 hazelnut brown

Anchor stranded cotton
J = 75 dusky pink

No. 8 straw (milliner's) needle
No. 8 crewel embroidery needle

EMBROIDERY KEY

All embroidery is worked with two strands of thread unless otherwise specified.

Boy with ball

Shorts = F (4 bullion knots, 7 - 11 wraps; 1 strand, couching)

Shirt = B (6 bullion knots, 7 - 12 wraps; 1 strand, couching)

Head = H (3 bullion knots, 8 - 9 wraps; 1 strand, couching)

Arm = H (bullion knot, 8 wraps)

Hand = H (French knot, 2 wraps)

Legs = H (3 strands, 1 bullion knot for each leg, 11 wraps; 1 strand, couching)

Shoes = F (1 bullion knot for each shoe, 5 wraps)

Hair = G (1 strand, French knot, 3 wraps)

Eye = E (1 strand, straight stitch)

Ball = C (2 bullion loops, 16 and 26 wraps, straight stitch; 1 strand, couching)

Girl with flowers

Dress = D (7 bullion knots, 7 - 21 wraps; 1 strand, couching)

Head = H (3 bullion knots, 7 - 9 wraps; 1 strand, couching)

Arm = H (bullion knot, 11 wraps)

Hand = H (French knot, 2 wraps)

Legs = H (3 strands, 1 bullion knot for each leg, 11 wraps; 1 strand, couching)

Shoes = J (1 bullion knot for each shoe, 5 wraps)

Hair = B (1 strand, straight stitch)

Eyes = E (1 strand, straight stitch)

Flower stems = D (1 strand, straight stitch, couching)

Flowers = A and J (1 strand, French knot, 2 wraps)

Girl Exercising

Pinafore = J (5 bullion knots, 16 - 18 wraps; 1 strand, couching)

Blouse = B (6 bullion knots, 6 - 8 wraps; 1 strand, couching)

Head = H (3 bullion knots, 8 - 9 wraps; 1 strand, couching)

Arms = H (1 bullion knot for each arm, 15 wraps; 1 strand, couching)

Hands = H (1 French knot for each hand, 2 wraps)

Legs = H (3 strands, 1 bullion knot for each leg, 11 wraps; 1 strand, couching)

Shoes = F (1 bullion knot for each shoe, 6 wraps)

Hair = I (French knot, 1 wrap)

Eyes = E (1 strand, straight stitch)

Boy doing handstand

Shorts = E (6 bullion knots, 6 wraps; 1 strand, couching)

Shirt = F (9 bullion knots, 5 - 13 wraps; 1 strand, couching)

Head = H (3 bullion knots, 8 - 9 wraps; 1 strand, couching)

Arms = H (1 bullion knot for each arm, 10 wraps; 1 strand, couching)

Hands = H (1 French knot for each hand, 2 wraps)

Legs = H (3 strands, 1 bullion knot for each leg, 11 wraps; 1 strand, couching)

Shoes = D (1 bullion knot for each shoe, 6 wraps)

Hair = G (1 strand, straight stitch)

Eyes = E (1 strand, straight stitch)

Child with balloons

Shorts = D (2 bullion knots, 9 and 13 wraps; 1 strand, couching)

Shirt = A (9 bullion knots, 4 - 11 wraps; 1 strand, couching)

Head = H (3 bullion knots, 8 - 9 wraps; 1 strand, couching)

Arms = H (1 bullion knot for each arm, 12 wraps; 1 strand, couching)

Hands = H (1 French knot for each hand, 2 wraps)

Legs = H (3 strands, 1 bullion knot for each leg, 16 wraps; 1 strand, couching)

Feet = H (3 strands, 1 bullion knot for each foot, 4 wraps)

Hair = B (1 strand, French knot, 3 wraps)

Eyes = E (1 strand, straight stitch)

Balloons

Strings = G (1 strand, back stitch)

Balloons = B, C or J (2 bullion loops for each balloon, 17 and 23 wraps; 1 strand, couching)

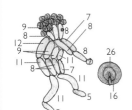

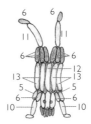
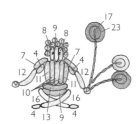

Icecreams

BY JENNY BROWN

REQUIREMENTS

White 100% cotton short sleeve body suit with binding trim

Threads & Needles
See page 37.

Supplies

11cm x 15cm wide (4 ⅜" x 6") piece of wax free transfer paper (eg. Saral) for neck and chest design

6cm x 5.5cm wide (2 ⅜" x 2 ¼") piece of wax free transfer paper (eg. Saral) for sleeve design

11cm x 15cm wide (4 ⅜" x 6") piece of heavy non-woven interfacing for neck and chest design

3cm x 5.5cm wide (1 ¼" x 2 ¼") piece of heavy non-woven interfacing for sleeve design

11cm x 15cm wide (4 ⅜" x 6") piece of cardboard for neck and chest design

3cm x 5.5cm wide (1 ¼" x 2 ¼") piece of cardboard for sleeve design

PREPARATION FOR EMBROIDERY

See the centre liftout pattern for the embroidery designs.

Neck and chest

Preparing the body suit
With the back of the shoulders, sleeves and side seams right sides together, fold the body suit down the length of the garment. Mark the centre front fold with a pin at the neckline and again 9.5cm (3 ¾") down from the top edge of the neck binding.

Transferring the embroidery design
Open the body suit out flat with the front uppermost. Place the larger piece of cardboard between the front and back neckline and chest area.

Trace the embroidery design and placement lines onto the larger piece of heavy interfacing. Place the larger piece of transfer paper, colour side down, onto the chest area of the body suit front. Place the interfacing, design side up, over the transfer paper. Ensure the placement marks on the tracing match the neckline and the pins on the body suit. Using a ball point pen and pressing firmly, trace the outlines of the ice creams and the lettering. Use dots to mark the positions of the cherries and the sprinkles on the neckline.

> Some people come into our lives and quickly go. Some stay for awhile, touch our hearts, and we are never, ever the same.
>
> ANONYMOUS

Sleeves

Mark the centre of one sleeve with a pin at the edge of the binding. Centre the smaller piece of cardboard inside the sleeve.

Cut the small piece of transfer paper into two pieces, each 3cm x 5.5cm wide (1 ¼" x 2 ¼"). Using a new piece of transfer paper for each sleeve, transfer the embroidery design for the sleeve in the same manner as the chest and neckline design, aligning the placement marks on the design with the pin and edges of the binding. Repeat for the remaining sleeve.

EMBROIDERY

Use the straw needle for working the bullion knots and the crewel needle for all other embroidery.

Order of Work
Cones
Outline the seven cones with back stitch. Fill the shape of each cone with six to eight diagonal rows of back stitch, angling the rows from the top right to the bottom left.

Icecream scoops
Stitch the scoops from the centre outwards, starting from the lower edge each time and varying the number of wraps according to the diagrams. Couch the knots in place with a single strand of matching thread.

Add French knot cherries and the chocolate bud to the icecreams following the diagram for placement.

Work the chocolate stick in the fifth icecream from the left hand side with two rows of chain stitch.

Lettering
Embroider the wording around the neckline and sleeves in back stitch, skimming through the top layers of fabric. When working the neckline, finish the thread for each word before beginning the next. Finally, add groups of three French knots between and at the ends of the words.

THIS DESIGN USES

Back stitch, Bullion knot, Chain stitch, Couching, French knot

THREADS & NEEDLES

DMC stranded cotton
A = 436 tan
B = 632 vy dk mocha
C = 744 lt yellow
D = 754 lt peach
E = 772 vy lt yellow-green
F = 775 baby blue
G = 3350 ultra dk dusky rose
H = 3716 vy lt dusky rose

Anchor stranded cotton
I = 129 lt delft blue

No. 8 straw (milliner's) needle
No. 8 crewel embroidery needle

EMBROIDERY KEY

All embroidery is worked with two strands of thread unless otherwise specified.

Note: The icecreams in the design are numbered from left to right.

Cones
Outline = A (1 strand, back stitch)
Filling = A (1 strand, back stitch)

Icecream 1
Scoop = E (3 bullion knots, 17 - 40 wraps; 1 strand, couching)
Chocolate bud = B (French knot, 3 wraps)

Icecream 2
Scoop = F (4 bullion knots, 5 - 40 wraps; 1 strand, couching)
Drips = F (2 bullion knots, 3 and 8 wraps)

Icecream 3
Scoop = H (4 bullion knots, 5 - 40 wraps; 1 strand, couching)
Cherries = G (French knot, 1 and 3 wraps)

Icecream 4
Large scoop = E (4 bullion knots, 5 - 40 wraps; 1 strand, couching)
Small scoop = C (3 bullion knots, 17 - 40 wraps; 1 strand, couching)
Cherry = G (French knot, 3 wraps)

Icecream 5
Scoop = D (4 bullion knots, 5 - 40 wraps; 1 strand, couching)
Chocolate stick = B (chain stitch)

Icecream 6
Spilt scoop = H (7 bullion knots, 8 - 28 wraps; 1 strand, couching)
Drip = H (bullion knot, 6 wraps)

Icecream 7
Large scoop = C (4 bullion knots, 5 - 40 wraps; 1 strand, couching)
Small scoop = F (3 bullion knots, 17 - 40 wraps; 1 strand, couching)
Cherry = G (French knot, 3 wraps)

Words = I (back stitch)

Sprinkles = C, D, E, F and H (French knot, 4 wraps)

Sleeve embroidery

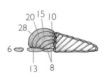

The finished embroidery design on the chest measures 2.5cm x 12.5cm wide (1" x 5")

THE
Christening Ensemble

by ALLA AKSELROD of VICTORIA

A priceless celebration

THE *Gown*

Christenings evoke feelings of wonder, peace, joy and splendour.
This graceful gown, with matching bonnet, shoes and bib will fill your heart with love and pride.

If making the gown, bonnet,
shoes and bib, 2.2m x 112cm wide
(2yd 14 ½" x 44") of fabric is required.

REQUIREMENTS FOR GOWN
SIZE 3 TO 6 MONTHS

Fabric

1.8m x 112cm wide (1yd 35" x 44")
white cotton voile

Threads, Ribbons & Needles

See page 44.

Supplies

1.4m x 5mm wide (1yd 19 ¼" x ³/₁₆")
double-sided satin ribbon for sleeve ties

50cm x 12mm wide (19 ¾" x ½")
white bias binding for sleeves

6 x 10mm wide (⅜") white buttons

25.5cm (10") embroidery hoop

15cm (6") embroidery hoop

0.5 mechanical lead pencil

Dressmaker's awl

PATTERN

See the centre liftout pattern.

The finished measurement of the gown from the centre back neckline to the hemline is 78.5cm (31").

CUTTING OUT & CONSTRUCTION

Trace the pattern pieces onto tracing paper or lightweight interfacing and transfer all pattern markings.

Cut out all pieces and assemble the gown following the cutting layout and construction details in the centre liftout pattern.

The gown is completely assembled before the embroidery is worked.

PREPARATION FOR EMBROIDERY

See the centre liftout pattern for the embroidery design.

Bodice

Trace the bodice embroidery design, including the stitch lines for the two centre tucks and the neckline, onto tracing paper. Position the tracing under the front of the gown, aligning the tuck stitch lines and the neckline on the gown with the stitch lines marked on the tracing. Pin in place to prevent movement.

Using the lead pencil, trace the outline for the eyelet border, the trailing ties and the tendrils. Mark the centres of the four-petalled flowers, side view roses, twirled ribbon roses and trailing buds and spots with dots. Draw fine lines to mark the placement of the rosebuds and the couched ribbon bow. Remove the tracing.

Skirt

Centre design

With wrong sides together, fold the lower front skirt in half to find the centre. Measuring up from the

hemline, press the fold for 30cm (11 ⅞"). Open out the front skirt. Measuring along the pressed fold line and beginning at the hemline, mark points at 6cm (2 ⅜") and 26cm (10¼"). These points are the positions of the spots above and below the design (*diag 1*).

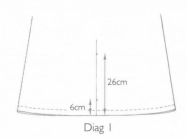

Diag I

THESE DESIGNS USE

Back stitch, Bullion knot,
Couching, Eyelets,
French knot, Granitos,
Loop stitch,
Padded satin stitch,
Satin stitch, Seed stitch,
Shadow work variation,
Stem stitch, Straight stitch,
Twirled ribbon rose

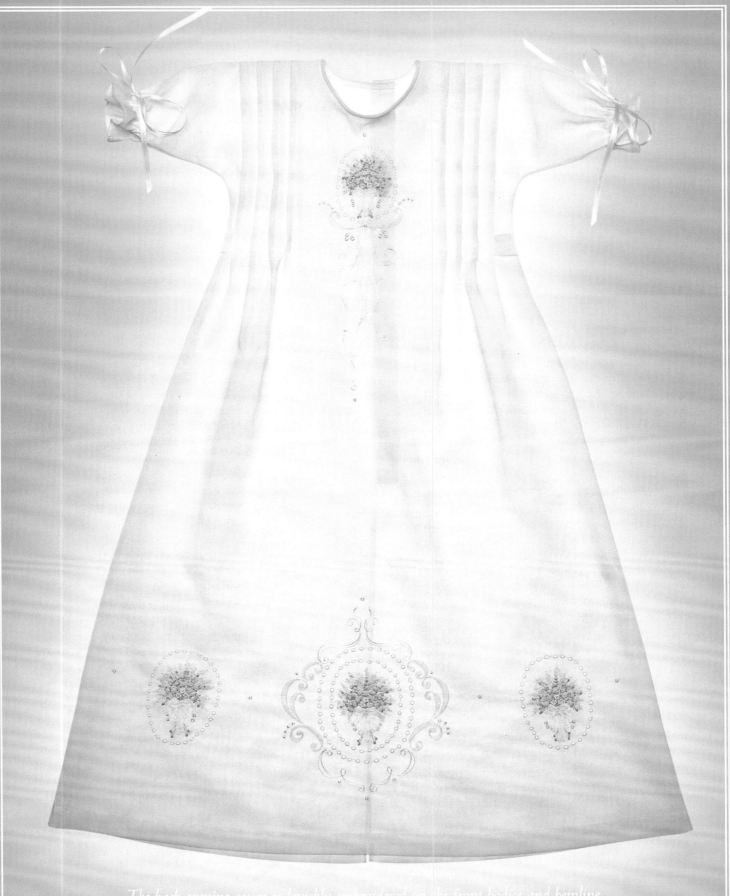

The back opening gown is lavishly embroidered on the front bodice and hemline.
Fabric sashes extend from the front tucks to tie at the back.

Trace the central skirt embroidery design onto tracing paper. Position the tracing under the lower front skirt, aligning the placement marks on the skirt with the spots on the design. Transfer the design in the same manner as the bodice.

Side designs
Beginning at the centre fold line, measure across 11cm (4 ¼") and 24.5cm (9 ⅝") to the left side seam. Mark both points with a pin. At these positions, measure up 16cm (6 ¼") from the hemline. Using the lead pencil, mark the points where the measurements meet. These points mark the position of the spots on each side of the design (*diag 2*).

Diag 2

24.5cm

11cm

16cm   16cm

Measure and mark the right hand side of the lower skirt in the same manner.

Trace the side skirt design onto tracing paper. Transfer the design to both sides of the lower skirt in the same manner as before.

EMBROIDERY

See page 17 for step-by-step instructions for granitos, page 45 for eyelets, page 49 for loop stitch, page 52 for shadow work variation and page 53 for twirled ribbon rose.

The intricate embroidery features a bouquet of four-petalled flowers, side view bullion roses, twirled ribbon roses, rosebuds and trailing padded satin stitch buds, tied with a couched ribbon bow. An oval medallion of eyelets linked with back stitches frame the bouquet.

On the bodice a trail of ties and tendrils falls gently into the skirt area.

The central design on the front skirt is framed with two ovals of eyelets surrounded by ornate shadow work scrolls and tendrils. On the side designs, repeat the bodice bouquet and single eyelet frame.

The straw needle is used for working the bullion knots. Use the no. 6 crewel needle for stitching the twirled ribbon roses. The no. 9 crewel needle is used for all other embroidery. Place the fabric in the hoop when working all embroidery except the bullion knots and stem stitching. Use the larger hoop when stitching the central design on the skirt and the smaller hoop for the remaining three designs.

Bodice

Eyelet medallion
Embroider the eyelets, working a connecting looped line of back stitches between them.

Bouquet
Stitch the large four-petalled flowers first. For each flower, stitch one petal followed by the opposite petal, rather than stitching around the flower. Stitch the remaining pair of petals and add the satin stitch centre.

Work the side view roses, starting with the centre bullion knot and working outwards. Position the two outer petals at the base of the rose.

Surround the bullion roses with seven small twirled ribbon roses. Stitch a French knot in the centre of each twirled ribbon rose, anchoring the ribbon at the same time.

Work a granitos with a bullion knot on each side for the three buds near the top of the bouquet. Embroider two bullion knots side by side for each remaining rosebud. Work the trailing buds in padded satin stitch.

Stitch the stems and leaves for the roses and rosebuds and surround the bouquet with scattered seed stitch and French knot specks. Embroider long straight stitches between the stems of the trailing buds and outline the buds and leaves using the metallic thread.

Ribbon bow
From the position for the bow knot, work a loop stitch measuring approximately 2.5cm (1") long. On each side, work a loop stitch measuring 2cm (¾") long. Finger press the loops downwards.

SPECIAL KIT OFFERS
from INSPIRATIONS BABY

THE *Receiving Shawl*
See page 4

Kit contains: Ivory winter twill, 11 stranded cottons, 2 embroidery needles, cream satin mini piping, non-fusible thin wadding

$59.00

FOR THE *Nursery*
See page 12

DOOR SWAG

Kit contains: Ivory cotton damask, ivory lightweight homespun, 4 crewel wools, 12 stranded cottons, 3 embroidery needles, ivory piping, polyester fibre-fill, ivory cotton ribbon, wax free transfer paper

$33.00

NAPPY PINCUSHION

Kit contains: Ivory cotton damask, ivory lightweight homespun, 5 crewel wools, 11 stranded cottons, 3 embroidery needles, ivory piping, polyester fibre-fill, covered buttons, wax free transfer paper

$33.00

THE *Bed Linen*
See page 20

Kit contains: White cotton voile, white cotton lace insertion, 7 stranded cottons, 1 stranded rayon, 2 embroidery needles, heirloom sewing thread

$49.00

Essential Undergarments
See page 26

Available in sizes OOO, OO, O and 1
Please indicate size required when ordering

'THE COW JUMPED OVER THE MOON'

Kit contains: White 100% cotton singlet or vest with lace trim, 6 stranded cottons, 2 embroidery needles, wax free transfer paper, interfacing, cardboard

$17.00

PLAY TIME

Kit contains: White 100% cotton short sleeve body suit with binding trim, 10 stranded cottons, 2 embroidery needles, wax free transfer paper interfacing, cardboard

$25.00

ICECREAMS

Kit contains: White 100% cotton short sleeve body suit, 9 stranded cottons, 2 embroidery needles, wax free transfer paper, interfacing, cardboard

$25.00

THE BUNNY

Kit contains: White 100% cotton singlet or vest with lace trim, 7 stranded cottons, 2 embroidery needles, wax free transfer paper, interfacing, cardboard

$17.00

---

*Please fill in the order form on the back of this coupon or phone your order direct on (08) 8364 1075
or fax: (08) 8364 0479 or email: cbumpkin@ozemail.com.au*

THE *Christening Ensemble*

Size 3 - 6 months
See page 38

ENSEMBLE
Kit contains:
White cotton voile,
2 cotton lace edgings,
8 stranded cottons,
2 stranded metallic
threads, 2 stranded
rayons, 1 silk ribbon,
3 embroidery needles,
satin ribbon,
bias binding,
buttons, satin mini
piping

$90.00

GOWN
Kit contains:
White cotton voile,
6 stranded cottons,
2 stranded metallic
threads,
2 stranded rayons,
1 silk ribbon,
3 embroidery needles,
satin ribbon, bias
binding, buttons

$60.00

BONNET
Kit contains:
White cotton voile,
cotton lace edging,
4 stranded cottons,
1 stranded rayon,
1 silk ribbon,
2 embroidery needles,
satin ribbon

$21.00

SHOES
Kit contains:
White cotton voile,
4 stranded cottons,
1 stranded rayon,

1 silk ribbon,
2 embroidery needles,
satin mini piping,
satin ribbon

$19.00

BIB
Kit contains: White
cotton voile, cotton
lace edging, 5 stranded
cottons, 2 stranded
rayons, 1 silk ribbon,
2 embroidery needles

$25.00

THE *Blanket*

See page 62

Kit contains: Ivory doctor's flannel, magnolia cathedral satin,
10 stranded cottons, 1 hand dyed 12 ply silk thread, 1 no. 3 perlé
cotton, 4 silk ribbons, 3 embroidery needles, interfacing

$88.00

Indispensable Accessories

See page 54   Please indicate size required when ordering.

FOR BABY GIRLS
Kit contains: Ivory featherwale
corduroy, pink featherwale
corduroy, batiste, ribbing,
flannelette, 8 stranded cottons,
2 embroidery needles, fine
piping cord, wadding, velcro

FOR BABY BOYS
Kit contains: Pale blue
featherwale corduroy, navy
featherwale corduroy, batiste,
ribbing, flannelette, 4 stranded
cottons, 1 embroidery needle,
fine piping cord, wadding, velcro

$36.00

$32.00

THE *First Dress*

Sizes 3, 6 and 12 months

See page 68

Kit contains: Pale pink Imperial batiste, lace edging,
5 stranded cottons, 2 embroidery needles, pearl buttons, interfacing

$40.00

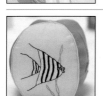

THE *Ball*

Kit contains: Scarlet poplin, orange
poplin, mint green poplin, aqua blue
poplin, 9 stranded cottons, 1 hand dyed
stranded cotton, 2 embroidery needles,

citron yellow mini piping,
interfacing, polyester
fibre-fill, cat's plastic
ball with bell

See page 76

$29.00

*Please fill in the order form on the back of this coupon or phone your order direct on (08) 8364 1075
or fax: (08) 8364 0479 or email: cbumpkin@ozemail.com.au*

ORDER FORM

PRICES INCLUDE P&H WITHIN AUSTRALIA ONLY
Prices on application for overseas orders.

INSPIRATIONS BABY ~ 1999
OFFICE USE ONLY
DATE REC'D
PAID
DATE SENT

☐ **I am a Country Bumpkin Club Member No.** _____

Page No.	Item No.	Description	Size	Q'ty	Price per item	Sub total

TOTAL | $

ORDERED BY *(please print clearly)*

Name _____

Address _____

_____

_____

State _____ Postcode/zip _____ Phone _____

HOW TO ORDER
Complete the order form and fax to:
(08) 8364 0479
OR post to: **REPLY PAID 18, CB Publications, PO Box 194, Kent Town SA 5071**
OR phone between 9am & 5pm (CST) weekdays on:
(08) 8364 1075 or FREECALL 1800 641 061
OR email to:
cbumpkin@ozemail.com.au

PAYMENT BY

☐ Visa ☐ Mastercard ☐ Bankcard ☐ Cheque ☐ M/order

*OVERSEAS CUSTOMERS PLEASE NOTE: We can only accept Visa, Mastercard, Bankcard or a bank draft in Australian dollars

CARD NUMBER

☐☐☐☐ ☐☐☐☐ ☐☐☐☐ ☐☐☐☐

EXPIRY DATE _____ / _____   SIGNATURE _____

IF YOU HAVE ENJOYED THIS BOOK YOU WILL LOVE OUR QUARTERLY PUBLICATIONS.

The world's most beautiful embroidery

INSPIRATIONS

At least eight wonderful embroidery projects, plus a detailed step-by-step stitch book. Full size liftout patterns.

More than just a magazine

AUSTRALIAN SMOCKING & EMBROIDERY

Glorious garments for all ages. Full size liftout patterns for all garments.

SUBSCRIBE TO *INSPIRATIONS* OR *AS&E* AND RECEIVE FOUR FABULOUS ISSUES A YEAR.
SUBSCRIBE TO BOTH AND RECEIVE EIGHT ISSUES A YEAR.

INSPIRATIONS
THE WORLD'S MOST BEAUTIFUL EMBROIDERY

NEW SUBSCRIPTION TO *Inspirations*

☐ **1 year subscription at A$36**
NZ & Pacific - A$56
Asia & Nth America - A$68
Other overseas - A$72

☐ **2 year subscription at A$72**
NZ & Pacific - A$112
Asia & Nth America - A$136
Other overseas - A$144

SMOCKING
AUSTRALIAN
& Embroidery

NEW SUBSCRIPTION TO *AS&E*

☐ **1 year subscription at A$34**
NZ & Pacific - A$54
Asia & Nth America - A$66
Other overseas - A$70

☐ **2 year subscription at A$68**
NZ & Pacific - A$108
Asia & Nth America - A$132
Other overseas - A$140

NAME *(please print clearly)* ....

Address ....

State .... Country .... Postcode .... Phone ....

I enclose a cheque/money order for A$ .... (payable to CB Publications)

[NOTE: ALL CHEQUES/MONEY ORDERS SHOULD BE IN AUSTRALIAN DOLLARS]

or please charge A$ .... to my credit card:

☐ Bankcard ☐ Visa ☐ MasterCard Signature ....

☐☐☐☐ ☐☐☐☐ ☐☐☐☐ ☐☐☐☐ Expiry date ..../........

Please tick if applicable

☐ Please renew this subscription automatically each year and charge my credit card. I understand I may cancel at any time and receive a refund of the unused portion of my subscription. I understand I will receive whichever subscription special offer is valid at time of renewing.

Signature ....

Using a piece of silk ribbon approximately 15cm (6") long, tie a bow with loops approximately 1cm (³⁄₈") long. Trim the ties to 3cm (1 ¼"). Fold the ties under to form two more loops. Secure the ends of the ribbon to the back of the bow knot. Position the bow to just cover the top of the three loop stitches and stitch in place. Couch all loops in place.

Ties and tendrils

Work the flowing ties at the base of the eyelet medallion using shadow work. Embroider the outlines in stem stitch first. Working on the wrong side of the fabric, fill in the shapes. Stitch from side to side, taking the needle and thread through the back of the stem stitches and not through the fabric.

Embroider the tendrils in stem stitch carrying the thread behind the shadow work ties where they cross over the tendrils.

Work the cream and white spots and trailing buds in padded satin stitch. Using the silver metallic thread, outline the buds and the spots above and below the design in back stitch. Stitch the stems to the white buds with long straight stitches.

Skirt

Central design

Embroider the two ovals of eyelets and the bouquet design in the same manner as the embroidery on the bodice. When stitching the fern, use straight stitches branching from a central line.

Work the scrolls in the same manner as the shadow embroidered ties and the stem stitched tendrils on the bodice.

Side designs

Stitch the bouquet and eyelet design in the same manner as the bodice.

Bodice embroidery

THREADS, RIBBONS & NEEDLES

DMC stranded cotton
A = blanc
B = ecru
C = 644 med beige-grey
D = 745 vy lt yellow
E = 818 baby pink
F = 3022 med Jacobean green

DMC stranded metallic thread
G = 5282 gold
H = 5283 silver

Anchor Marlitt stranded rayon
I = 800 white
J = 1212 cream

YLI pure silk ribbon 4mm
(³⁄₁₆") wide
K = 2.5m (2yd 26 ½")
no. 1 antique white

No. 6 crewel embroidery needle
No. 9 crewel embroidery needle
No. 9 straw (milliner's) needle

EMBROIDERY KEY

All thread embroidery is worked with one strand unless otherwise specified.

Oval medallions = A (eyelets, back stitch)

Bouquet
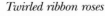
Large four-petalled flowers
Centre = D (satin stitch)
Petals = B (2 strands, padding),
J (satin stitch)

Small four-petalled flowers on bodice and centre skirt designs only
Centre = D (satin stitch)
Petals = J (granitos)

Side view roses
Centre = J (bullion knot, 6 wraps)
Inner petals = A (2 bullion knots, 8 wraps)
Outer petals = A (4 bullion knots, 12 - 14 wraps)
Calyx = C, F and G, or H (straight stitch)
Stamen = C and F (straight stitch)

Twirled ribbon roses
Petals = K (twirled ribbon rose)
Centre = B or E (French knot, 1 - 2 wraps)

Rosebuds
Centre = J (granitos) or none
Outer petals = A (2 bullion knots, 6 wraps)
Calyx = C and F (straight stitch)
Stamen = C and F (straight stitch)

Trailing buds
White buds = A (padding), I (satin stitch)
Stems = A and I (straight stitch)
Outlines = H (back stitch)

Green buds = C (granitos)
Outlines = F or H (straight stitch)
Stems = C and F (straight stitch)

Leaves = C and F (granitos, straight stitch)
Leaf highlights = H (back stitch)

Specks = A (2 strands, seed stitch, French knot, 1 wrap), G (seed stitch)

Fern on centre skirt design only
Fronds = C (straight stitch)

Bow = K (tied bow, loop stitch), B (couching)

Spots
Cream spots = B (2 strands, padding), J (satin stitch)
White spots = A (2 strands, padding), I (satin stitch)
Outlines on white spots = H (back stitch) or none

Trailing ties
Ties = A (stem stitch), A (2 strands, shadow work)
Tendrils = A and J (stem stitch)

Scroll
Scroll = A (stem stitch), A (2 strands, shadow work), A and J (stem stitch)

Centre motif on skirt

Eyelets have a small central hole, which is surrounded by running stitches and then covered by short, regular, overcasting stitches. For the step-by-step photographs we used two strands of stranded cotton and contrasting thread.

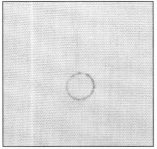

1. Mark the position for the eyelet with a small circle.

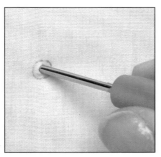

2. With the right side of the fabric facing you and using a dressmaker's awl, pierce the fabric at the centre of the marked circle. The awl should carefully separate the fabric fibres.

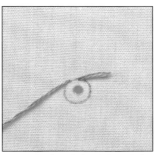

3. With the right side of the fabric facing and beginning on the marked line, work a small running stitch. Pull the thread through, leaving a tail of approx 3mm (⅛").

4. Work small running stitches around the circle. On the last stitch, take the needle through the first stitch, splitting the stitch. Pull the thread through.

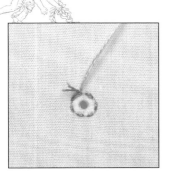

5. Re-pierce the hole with the awl. Bring the needle and thread to the front of the work just outside a running stitch.

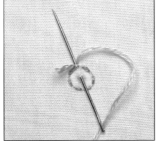

6. Take the needle through the pierced hole and bring it to the right side of the fabric directly alongside the emerging thread.

7. Pull the thread through. Holding the emerging thread, take the needle through the pierced hole and bring it to the front alongside the previous stitch.

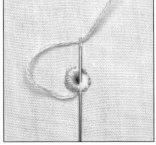

8. Closely overcast the edge of the eyelet. Keep turning the work to maintain a consistent fanning of the stitches. Keep an even tension on the closely worked stitches.

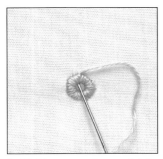

9. Finish overcasting and take the thread to the back through the hole.

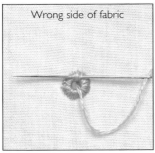
Wrong side of fabric

10. To end off, take the thread under the overcast stitches on the back.

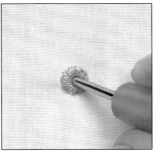

11. If necessary, use the awl to carefully re-pierce the hole from the back. This helps to 'settle' the thread and fabric.

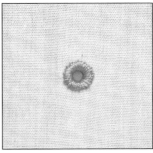

12. **Completed eyelet.**

The finished bonnet is designed to fit

a baby's head approximately 44 - 45cm (17 ¼ - 17 ⅝ ") in circumference.

REQUIREMENTS FOR BONNET

Fabric & Lace

25cm x 112cm wide (9 ¾" x 44")
piece of white cotton voile

1.1m x 15mm wide (1yd 7" x ⅝")
white cotton lace edging

Threads, Ribbons & Needles

See this page.

Supplies

80cm x 5mm wide (31 ½" x ³/₁₆")
white double-sided satin ribbon for ties

0.5 mechanical lead pencil

PREPARATION FOR EMBROIDERY

*See the centre liftout pattern for the
cutting layout, pattern pieces and
embroidery design.*

Trace the pattern pieces onto tracing
paper or lightweight interfacing and
transfer all pattern markings, including
the embroidery design. Following the
cutting layout in the centre liftout
pattern, cut out all the pieces which do
not require embroidery.

Position the front band pattern piece
under the fabric. Pin in place. Using
the lead pencil, trace all pattern
markings and the outlines for the
tendrils. Mark the centres of the four-
petalled flowers, the side view rose and
the spots with dots. Draw fine lines to
mark the placement of the rosebuds.
Unpin the pattern piece. Do not cut
out the piece to the exact shape until
after the embroidery is worked.

EMBROIDERY

The centre front of the bonnet band is
delicately embroidered with a pretty
bouquet. A tied ribbon bow is couched
at the base of the design. Two rosebuds
are worked across the band on each
side of the central bouquet.

Use the straw needle for the bullion
knots and the crewel needle for all
other embroidery.

Order of Work

Bouquet

Work the petals of the four-petalled
flowers with padded satin stitch and
add the yellow centres. Embroider
the single side view bullion rose,
followed by the rosebuds. Add
trailing tendrils on each side of
the bouquet.

Embroider the foliage, using straight
stitches of varying lengths for the
stamens and calyx of each rose and
rosebud.

Work the scattered white specks with
seed stitch or French knots and
add padded satin stitch spots among
the tendrils.

Ribbon bow

Using the antique white silk ribbon,
tie a bow with loops approximately
8mm (⁵/₁₆") long. Trim the ties to
2.5cm (1") long. Fold the ties under to
form two more loops. Secure the ends
of the ties to the back of the bow knot.
Position the bow just below the four-
petalled flowers and couch in place.

Single rosebuds

Stitch two rosebuds on each side of the
bouquet. Add a pair of straight stitches
at each end of the buds for leaves.

CONSTRUCTION

See the centre liftout pattern.

THREADS, RIBBONS & NEEDLES

DMC stranded cotton
A = blanc
B = 524 vy lt fern green
C = 644 med beige-grey
D = 745 vy lt yellow

Anchor Marlitt stranded rayon
E = 800 white

YLI pure silk ribbon 4mm (³/₁₆") wide
F = 15cm (6") no. 1 antique white

No. 9 crewel embroidery needle
No. 9 straw (milliner's) needle

— EMBROIDERY KEY —
for the BONNET

*All thread embroidery is worked with one
strand unless otherwise specified.*

Bouquet

Four-petalled flowers
Petals = A (2 strands, padding),
E (satin stitch)

Centre = D (satin stitch)

Side view rose
Centre = A (2 strands, 2 bullion
knots, 9 wraps)

Outer petals = A (2 strands,
4 bullion knots, 8 - 12 wraps)

Rosebuds
Petals = A (2 strands, 2 bullion
knots, 6 wraps)

Stems and leaves = B or C
(straight stitch)

Tendrils = E (stem stitch)

Spots = A (2 strands,
padded satin stitch)

Specks = A (2 strands,
seed stitch, French knot, 1 wrap)

Ribbon bow = F (tied bow),
A (couching)

Single rosebuds
Petals = A (2 strands,
2 bullion knots, 9 wraps)

Leaves = B (straight stitch)

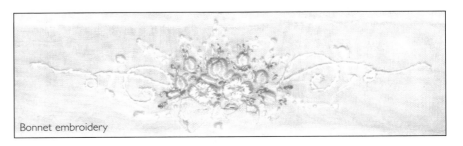

Bonnet embroidery

THE *Shoes*

── The finished shoe is designed for a little foot 10cm (4") long ──

REQUIREMENTS FOR SHOES

Fabric
25cm x 112cm wide (9 ¾" x 44") piece of white cotton voile

Threads, Ribbons & Needles
See page 49.

Supplies
70cm (27 ½") white satin mini piping

1m x 5mm wide (39 ½" x ³⁄₁₆") double-sided satin ribbon for ties

0.5 mechanical lead pencil

PREPARATION FOR EMBROIDERY

See the centre liftout pattern for the cutting layout, pattern pieces and embroidery design.

Trace the pattern pieces onto tracing paper or lightweight interfacing and transfer all pattern markings, including the embroidery design. Following the cutting layout, cut out all the pieces which do not require embroidery.

Transfer the pattern markings and embroidery designs to the toe pieces following the procedure used for the bonnet. Do not cut out the piece to the exact shape until after the embroidery is worked.

EMBROIDERY

See page 17 for step-by-step instructions for granitos.

The toe of each little shoe is embroidered with a single four-petalled flower centred between two bullion roses. Three rosebuds are positioned above the four-petalled flower. Padded satin stitch buds fall gently below the tied bow which holds the spray.

Use the straw needle for the bullion knots and the crewel needle for all other embroidery.

Order of Work

Bouquet
Work the four-petalled flower, followed by the side view roses on each side. Stitch the rosebuds next.

Embroider the trailing buds and stems. Work the foliage with straight stitches of varying sizes and scatter the seed stitch and French knot specks.

Ribbon bow
Using the silk ribbon, tie a bow with loops approximately 8mm (⁵⁄₁₆") long. Trim the ties to 2.5cm (1"). Fold the ties under to form two more loops. Secure the ends of the ties to the back of the bow knot. Couch the bow just below the four-petalled flower.

White spots
Embroider two white spots on each side of the bouquet with granitos.

CONSTRUCTION
See the centre liftout pattern.

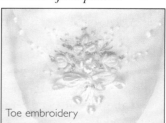
Toe embroidery

LOOP STITCH

Loop stitch is a three-dimensional stitch, usually worked in ribbon.

It is important to secure the ribbon on the back of the fabric with tiny stitches as this is a stitch which can easily be snagged.

For the step-by-step photogra (³⁄₁₆") wide ribbon.

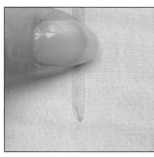

1. Leaving a 1cm (³⁄₈") tail of ribbon on the back of the fabric, bring the ribbon to the front at A. Secure the tail of ribbon with matching machine sewing thread.

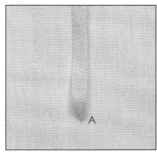

2. Hold the ribbon flat on the fabric with your left thumb.

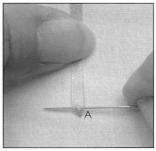

3. Place the needle under the ribbon near A. Using a slight upward pressure, move the needle towards your thumb to flatten the ribbon.

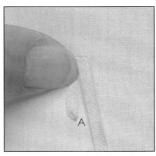

4. Keeping your left thumb on the ribbon, fold it over and back towards A, forming a loop.

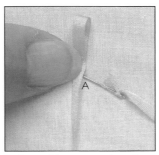

5. Reposition your thumb to hold both layers of ribbon in place. Take the needle to back of fabric next to A, ensuring the ribbon does not twist.

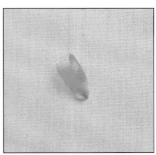

6. Gently pull the ribbon through until the loop is the desired size. **Completed loop stitch.**

EMBROIDERY KEY *for the* SHOES

THREADS, RIBBONS & NEEDLES

DMC stranded cotton
A = blanc
B = 524 vy lt fern green
C = 644 med beige-grey
D = 745 vy lt yellow

Anchor Marlitt stranded rayon
E = 800 white

YLI pure silk ribbon 4mm (³⁄₁₆") wide
F = 30cm (11 ³⁄₄") no. 1 antique white

No. 9 crewel embroidery needle
No. 9 straw (milliner's) needle

EMBROIDERY KEY

All thread embroidery is worked with one strand unless otherwise specified.

Bouquet
Four-petalled flower
Petals = A (2 strands, padding), E (satin stitch)
Centre = D (satin stitch)

Side view rose
Centre = A (2 strands, 2 bullion knots, 9 wraps)
Outer petals = A (2 strands, 4 bullion knots, 8 - 12 wraps)

Rosebuds
Petals = A (2 strands, 2 bullion knots, 6 wraps)
Trailing buds = A (2 strands, padding), E (satin stitch)
Stems and leaves = B or C (straight stitch)
Specks = A (2 strands, seed stitch, French knot, 1 wrap)
Ribbon bow = F (tied bow), A (couching)
Spots = A 2 strands, granitos)

REQUIREMENTS FOR BIB

Fabric & Lace

*30cm x 112cm wide (11 ¾" x 44")
piece of white cotton voile*

*1.3m x 12mm wide (1yd 15" x ½")
white cotton lace edging*

Threads, Ribbons & Needles

See page 51.

Supplies

0.5 mechanical lead pencil

PREPARATION FOR EMBROIDERY

*See the centre liftout pattern for the
cutting layout, pattern pieces and
embroidery design.*

Trace the pattern pieces onto tracing
paper or lightweight interfacing and
transfer all the pattern markings.
Following the cutting layout, cut out
the lining piece which does not need
embroidery. For the front piece and
interlining, cut two pieces, each 30cm
x 25cm wide (11 ¾" x 9 ¾").

Using the lead pencil, transfer the
pattern markings and embroidery
design to the front in the same
manner as the bonnet.

Trace the outline for the tendrils and
trailing white buds. Mark the centres
of the four-petalled flowers, the side
view roses and the spots with dots.
Draw fine lines to mark the
placement of the rosebuds and the
tied ribbon bow.

Do not cut out the piece to the exact
shape until after the embroidery has
been worked. With wrong sides
together, place the marked front over
the interlining piece and tack together
1.5cm (⅝") in from the marked
cutting line. Treat as a single layer.

EMBROIDERY

*See page 17 for step-by-step instructions
for granitos.*

A spray of delicate flowers is held
with a soft ribbon bow. Tendrils,
trailing buds and scattered spots flow
from the design.

Use the straw needle for the bullion
knots and the crewel needle for all
other embroidery.

Order of Work

Bouquet

Work the two large four-petalled
flowers and surround them with three
side view roses. Add the bullion

rosebuds next. Stitch the flowing
tendrils with stem stitch. Embroider
the large white padded satin stitch
buds and work the straight stitch
stems. Add the foliage, the small four-
petalled flowers near the edges of the
spray and then the white specks.

Ribbon bow

From the position for the bow knot,
work a loop stitch approximately
2.5cm (1") long. On each side, work
a loop stitch 2cm (¾") long. Finger
press the loops downwards.

Using the remaining length of silk
ribbon, tie a bow with loops approximately 1cm (⅜") long. Trim the ties
to 3cm (1 ¼"). Fold the ties under to
form two more loops. Secure the
ends of the ties to the back of the bow
knot. Position the bow to just cover
the top of the three loop stitches
and stitch in place. Couch all loops
in place.

White spots

Finally, stitch three white spots on
each side of the design and one spot
at the top and bottom.

CONSTRUCTION

See the centre liftout pattern.

THREADS, RIBBONS & NEEDLES

DMC stranded cotton
A = blanc
B = ecru
C = 524 vy lt fern green
D = 644 med beige-grey
E = 745 vy lt yellow

Anchor Marlitt stranded rayon
F = 800 white
G = 1212 cream

YLI pure silk ribbon 4mm (³⁄₁₆") wide
H = 35cm (13 ¾") no. 1 antique white

No. 9 crewel embroidery needle
No. 9 straw (milliner's) needle

EMBROIDERY KEY

All thread embroidery is worked with one strand unless otherwise specified.

Bouquet

Large four-petalled flowers
Petals = B (2 strands, padding), G (satin stitch)

Centre = E (satin stitch)

Small four-petalled flowers
Petals = F (granitos)

Side view rose
Centre = B (2 strands, bullion knot, 6 wraps)

Inner petals = A (2 strands, 2 bullion knots, 4 - 5 wraps)
Outer petals = A (2 strands, 4 bullion knots, 8 - 11 wraps)

Rosebuds
Petals = A or B (2 strands, 2 bullion knots, 6 wraps)

Trailing buds
Cream buds = B (2 strands, padding), G (satin stitch)
Stems of cream buds = B (2 strands, straight stitch), or C (straight stitch)
Green buds = C (granitos)
Stems of green buds = C (straight stitch)

Scattered stems and leaves = C and D (straight stitch)

Tendrils = A or B (stem stitch)

Specks = A (2 strands, seed stitch, French knot, 1 wrap)

Ribbon bow = H (tied bow, loop stitch), A (couching)

Spots = A (2 strands, granitos)

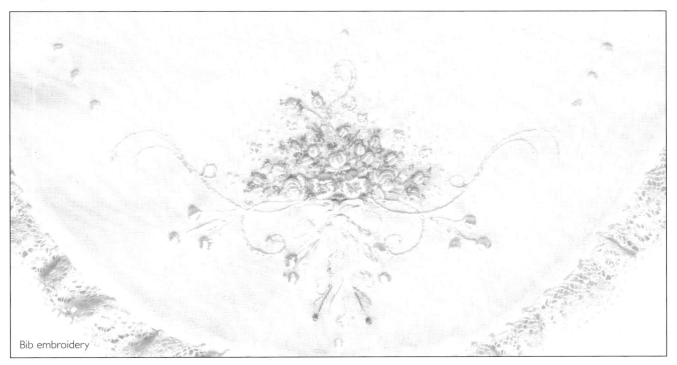

Bib embroidery

The finished bib is 12cm (4 ³⁄₄") deep at the centre front

SHADOW WORK VARIATION

This variation of shadow embroidery is worked in two stages and uses a combination of back stitch and detached herringbone stitch. If you wish, two shades of thread can be used - a lighter one on the front of the fabric and a darker one on the back. For the step-by-step photographs we used two strands of stranded cotton.

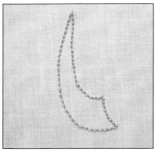

1. Back stitch outline. Mark the outline on the fabric. Back stitch along the outline, taking stitches approximately 2mm (1/16") long.

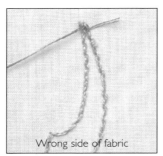

Wrong side of fabric

2. Detached herringbone stitch. Turn the fabric to the wrong side. Anchor a new thread near the top right hand side of the shape with 2 - 3 tiny back stitches through the stitching.

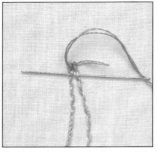

3. Slide the needle from right to left under the stitch near the secured thread and then under a stitch on the opposite side. Do not go through the fabric.

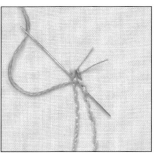

4. Pull the thread through. Slide the needle from left to right under the stitch directly above and then under the stitch on the opposite side which is directly below the previously used stitch.

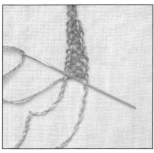

5. Pull the thread through. Slide the needle from left to right through the stitch directly above and then under the stitch on the opposite side just below the previously used stitch. Continue, keeping stitches at right angles to sides.

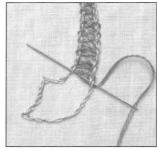

6. Working a curve. Going in the opposite direction to the previous stitch, slide needle under stitch directly above on the outer curve. On the opposite side (inner curve), take needle under same stitch as last stitch used.

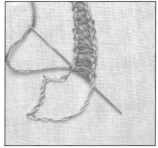

7. Pull the thread through. Going in the opposite direction to the previous stitch, slide the needle under the stitch directly above, then under the next unused stitch on the outer curve.

8. Continue working around the curve in the same manner. On the inner curve, periodically use the same stitch so the stitches remain roughly at right angles to the sides of the shape.

9. When reaching a straight section of the shape, work in the same manner using a new stitch on both sides of the shape for each stitch.

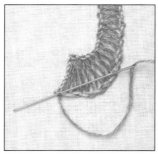

10. To end off, work 2 - 3 tiny back stitches through the outline on the back of the fabric.

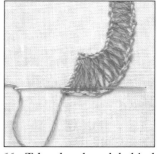

11. Take the thread behind some of the detached herringbone stitches close to the outline for approx. 1cm (3/8") and trim any excess thread.

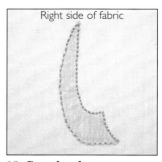

Right side of fabric

12. Completed shadow work on the right side of the fabric.

TWIRLED RIBBON ROSE

The special effect of a twirled ribbon rose is achieved by twisting the ribbon tightly as the rose is formed. The result is a firmly wound, soft ribbon rose. Before you begin, thread a needle with matching machine sewing thread. For the step-by-step photograph we used 7mm (⁵⁄₁₆") wide ribbon and contrasting machine sewing thread.

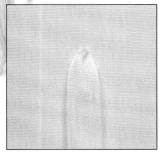

1. Secure the ribbon on the back of the fabric. Bring it to the front at the position for the centre of the rose (A).

2. Hold the needle up so the ribbon is taut and vertical to the fabric. Begin to twist the needle in an anti-clockwise direction.

3. Continue twirling the needle until the ribbon is tightly twisted.

4. Test the amount of twist by gently easing the tension on the ribbon. If it is wound tightly enough, it will buckle.

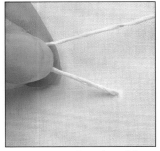

5. Using your thumb and forefinger, grasp the twisted ribbon approximately 3cm (1 ¼") from the fabric.

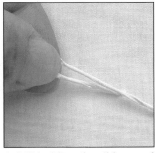

6. Still holding the ribbon and keeping it taut, fold it over to form a loop.

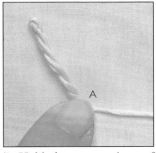

7. Hold the two sections of ribbon together close to A. Release the folded end. The ribbon will twist around itself forming a double coil.

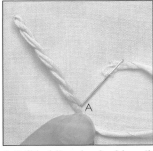

8. Still holding the double coil, take the needle to the back of the fabric just next to A.

9. Pull the ribbon through until reaching the doubled coil.

10. Continue pulling gently until the rose is the desired size.

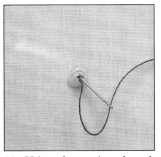

11. Using the sewing thread, secure the rose with two tiny stitches near the centre. Place the stitches so they are as invisible as possible.

12. Trim the ribbon on the back of the fabric to 1cm (³⁄₈"). Secure the ribbon with the thread and end off. **Completed twirled ribbon rose.**

INDISPENSABLE ACCESSORIES BY SHARON VENHOEK OF SOUTH AUSTRALIA

For Baby Girls

Soul-warming additions to your little one's wardrobe.
The hat, shoes and bib are made of the softest featherwale corduroy.

REQUIREMENTS
SIZES SMALL, MEDIUM & LARGE

Fabric

HAT - FOR ALL SIZES

20cm x 80cm wide (8" x 31 ½")
piece of ivory featherwale corduroy

20cm x 80cm wide (8" x 31 ½")
piece of ivory batiste for lining

9cm x 40cm wide (3 ½" x 15 ¾")
piece of ivory ribbing

35cm (13 ¾") square of pink featherwale
corduroy for trim

SHOES - FOR ALL SIZES

20cm x 112cm wide (8" x 44")
piece of ivory featherwale corduroy

40cm x 45cm wide (15 ¾" x 17 ¾")
piece of pink featherwale corduroy for trim

BIB

40cm x 50cm wide (15 ¾" x 19 ¾")
piece of ivory featherwale corduroy

40cm x 25cm wide (15 ¾" x 9 ⅞")
piece of white flannelette for interlining

35cm x 45cm wide (13 ¾" x 17 ¾")
piece of pink featherwale corduroy for trim

Note: If making all three items you
will need

55cm x 112cm wide (21 ¾" x 44")
ivory featherwale corduroy

45cm x 60cm wide (17 ¾" x 23 ⅝")
pink featherwale corduroy for trim

20cm x 80cm wide (8" x 31 ½")
piece of ivory batiste for hat lining

9cm x 40cm wide (3 ½" x 15 ¾")
piece of ivory ribbing

40cm x 25cm wide (15 ¾" x 9 ⅞")
*piece of white flannelette for bib
interlining*

3m (3yd 10") fine piping cord

Threads & Needles
See page 57.

Supplies

80cm (31 ½") fine piping cord for hat

90cm (35 ½") fine piping cord for shoes

1.3m (1yd 15") fine piping cord for bib

15cm x 90cm wide (6" x 35 ½")
*piece of fusible thin wadding
(eg. Pellon) for shoes*

6cm x 2.5cm wide (2 ⅜" x 1")
piece of white velcro for bib

Water-soluble fabric marker

PATTERN

See the centre liftout pattern.

The hat is designed to fit a head
circumference of
Small: 40 - 42cm (15 ¾ - 16 ½")
Medium: 43 - 45cm (16 ⅞ - 17 ¾")
Large: 46 - 48cm (18 ⅛ - 18 ⅞")

The shoes are designed for a foot
length of
Small: 10cm (3 ⅞")
Medium: 11cm (4 ¼")
Large: 12cm (4 ⅝")

The bib is 16.8cm (6 ⅝") deep at
the centre front for all sizes.

CUTTING OUT

*See the centre liftout pattern for the
cutting layout.*

Using a black pen, trace the pattern
pieces onto lightweight interfacing
or tracing paper and transfer all
pattern markings. Following the
cutting layout, cut out all pieces
which do not require embroidery.
For the remaining pieces, transfer
the pattern markings, but do not cut
them to the exact shape until after
the embroidery has been worked.

PREPARATION FOR EMBROIDERY

*See the centre liftout pattern for the
embroidery designs.*

Hat

Trace the embroidery designs, including the placement lines, onto tracing
paper. Tape the tracing to a window or
lightbox. With the right side facing
you, position one hat panel over the
tracing. Align the placement lines on
the hat with the marked lines on the
tracing. Tape in place. The light
shining through will make the design
visible through the fabric.

Using the fabric marker and in both
designs, mark the centres of the bullion
roses and French knot daisies with
dots. Mark the positions of the leaves
with small lines. Remove the tracing.
Following the same procedure, transfer
the single rose spray only to the three
remaining hat panels.

Shoes

Transfer the two embroidery designs
to each toe in the same manner as
the hat.

Bib

Transfer the embroidery design to
the lower edge of the bib front in the
same manner as the hat.

"Of course. A girl. I feel I have always known her always, always my girl."

"So it's you" I whisper. "So it's you, Rebecca."

A N N A   M A R I A   D E L L

EMBROIDERY

Use the straw needle for the bullion and French knots and the crewel needle for all other embroidery.

Order of Work

Hat

On the upper design, work the side view rose first. Using the darkest pink thread, stitch the centre two bullion knots. Change to the lighter thread and work three bullion knots for the inner petals. Surrounding the base of the rose and using the lightest shade of pink, add five bullion knots for the outer petals.

Embroider a blue forget-me-not on each side of the rose, using a yellow French knot for the centre surrounded by five blue French knots for the petals.

Scatter detached chain leaves among the flowers, using the three shades of green thread.

Vary the length of the anchoring stitch to create a leaf with an elongated appearance.

Embroider the remaining three panels in the same manner.

On the lower design of the centre front panel, embroider the full blown rose first. Begin with the centre two bullion knots, then work the three inner petals. Add the six outer petals, positioning them evenly around the inner petals. Working out from the middle, stitch the side view roses, forget-me-nots and leaves in the same manner as the upper design.

Shoes

Work the single side view rose at the top of the shoe and add detached chain leaves. Stitch the central full blown rose on the toe of the shoe. Work the side view roses in the same manner as before.

Embroider a French knot forget-me-not between each rose and at each end of the spray.

Scatter detached chain leaves around the flowers, positioning the colours in a similar manner as the hat. Repeat for the second shoe.

Bib

Begin the middle group of three roses by working the central full blown rose followed by a side view rose on each side. Work a pair of side view roses to the left and right of the middle group. Add a side view rose near each end. Embroider blue forget-me-nots between the groups of roses. Scatter green detached chain leaves among the flowers as before.

CONSTRUCTION

See the centre liftout pattern.

E M B R O I D E R Y   K E Y *for the* B A B Y   G I R L   A C C E S S O R I E S

THREADS & NEEDLES

DMC stranded cotton

A = *744 lt yellow*

B = *800 pale delft*

C = *963 ultra lt dusky rose*

D = *3013 lt khaki green*

E = *3022 med Jacobean green*

F = *3024 vy lt Jacobean green*

G = *3716 vy lt dusky rose*

H = *3733 dusky rose*

No. 9 crewel embroidery needle

No. 9 straw (milliner's) needle

THESE DESIGNS USE

Bullion knot, Detached chain,

French knot, Straight stitch,

Back stitch, Couching

EMBROIDERY KEY

All embroidery is worked with two strands of thread unless otherwise specified.

Full blown rose

Centre = H (2 bullion knots, 7 wraps)

Inner petals = G (3 bullion knots, 12 wraps)

Outer petals = C (6 bullion knots, 12 wraps)

Side view rose

Centre = H (2 bullion knots, 7 wraps)

Inner petals = G (3 bullion knots, 12 wraps)

Outer petals = C (5 bullion knots, 14 wraps)

Forget-me-nots

Centre = A (French knot, 2 wraps)

Petals = B (5 French knots, 2 wraps)

Leaves = D, E, and F (detached chain)

Crown embroidery

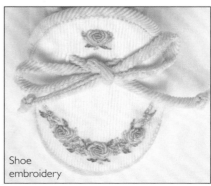

Shoe embroidery

For Baby Boys

There's a garden that I ken, Full of little gentlemen;

Little caps of blue they wear, And green ribbons, very fair.

f r o m STORIES TO TELL TO CHILDREN *by* SARA CONE BRYANT

REQUIREMENTS

SIZES SMALL, MEDIUM & LARGE

Fabric

HAT - FOR ALL SIZES

*20cm x 80cm wide (8" x 31 ½")
piece of pale blue featherwale corduroy*

*20cm x 80cm wide (8" x 31 ½")
piece of blue batiste for lining*

*9cm x 40cm wide (3 ½" x 15 ¾")
piece of pale blue ribbing*

*35cm (13 ¾") square of navy
featherwale corduroy for trim*

SHOES - FOR ALL SIZES

*20cm x 112cm wide (8" x 44")
piece of pale blue featherwale corduroy*

*40cm x 45cm wide (15 ¾" x 17 ¾")
piece of navy featherwale corduroy for trim*

BIB

*40cm x 50cm wide (15 ¾" x 19 ¾")
piece of pale blue featherwale corduroy*

*40cm x 25cm wide (15 ¾" x 9 ⅞")
piece of white flannelette for interlining*

*35cm x 45cm wide (13 ¾" x 17 ¾")
piece of navy featherwale corduroy for trim*

Note: If making all three items you
will need

*55cm x 112cm wide (21 ¾" x 44")
pale blue featherwale corduroy*

*45cm x 60cm wide (17 ¾" x 23 ⅝")
navy featherwale corduroy for trim*

*20cm x 80cm wide (8" x 31 ½")
piece of blue batiste for hat lining*

*9cm x 40cm wide (3 ½" x 15 ¾")
piece of pale blue ribbing*

*40cm x 25cm wide (15 ¾" x 9 ⅞") piece
of white flannelette for bib interlining*

3m (3yd 10") fine piping cord

Threads & Needles

See page 61.

Supplies

80cm (31 ½") fine piping cord for hat

90cm (35 ½") fine piping cord for shoes

1.3m (1yd 15") fine piping cord for bib

*15cm x 90cm wide (6" x 35 ½") piece
of fusible thin wadding (eg. Pellon)
for shoes*

*6cm x 2.5cm wide (2 ⅜" x 1")
piece of white velcro for bib*

Water-soluble fabric marker

PATTERN

See the centre liftout pattern.

The hat is designed to fit a head
circumference of
Small: 40 - 42cm (15 ¾ - 16 ½")
Medium: 43 - 45cm (16 ⅞ - 17 ¾")
Large: 46 - 48cm (18 ⅛ - 18 ⅞")

The shoes are designed for a foot
length of
Small: 10cm (3 ⅞")
Medium: 11cm (4 ¼")
Large: 12cm (4 ⅝")

The bib is 16.8cm (6 ⅝") deep at
the centre front for all sizes.

CUTTING OUT

*See the centre liftout pattern for the
cutting layout.*

Using a black pen, trace the pattern
pieces onto lightweight interfacing or
tracing paper and transfer all pattern
markings. Following the cutting layout,
cut out all pieces which do not require
embroidery. For the remaining pieces,
transfer the pattern markings, but do
not cut them to the exact shape until
after the embroidery has been worked.

PREPARATION FOR EMBROIDERY

*See the centre liftout pattern for the
embroidery designs.*

Hat

Trace the embroidery design including
the placement lines onto tracing paper.
Tape the tracing to a window or
lightbox. With the right side facing you,
position one hat panel over the tracing.
Align the placement lines on the hat
with the marked lines on the tracing.
Tape in place. The light shining
through will make the design visible
through the fabric.

Such a little body, Such a big miracle. ~ J U D Y   F O R D

Using the fabric marker, trace the outline for the steam train. Remove the tracing.

Shoes

Transfer the embroidery design to one toe in the same manner as the hat. Flip the tracing over and transfer a mirror imaged steam train to the second toe.

Bib

Transfer the embroidery design to the lower edge of the bib front in the same manner as the hat.

EMBROIDERY

All steam trains are stitched in exactly the same manner. Use the no. 9 straw needle for all embroidery.

Order of Work

Work the steam train following the diagram for the number of wraps required. Beginning with the driver's compartment, work the bullion knots in the navy thread, varying the number of wraps according to the diagram. Using the garnet thread, work twelve bullion knots for the engine. Change to the sky blue thread and stitch the bullion knots for the chassis, the engine front and the compartment roof. Couch the longest knot in place. Add the smoke stacks with the black thread.

Stitch the black buffers with two horizontal straight stitches, then work a single vertical straight stitch at the end. Embroider the wheels using closely packed straight stitches. Outline each wheel in back stitch and add a single wrap French knot to the centre. Link the wheels with a straight stitch between each French knot.

Finally, on the engine, work a tiny black French knot on every alternate bullion knot to add detail.

CONSTRUCTION

See the centre liftout pattern.

EMBROIDERY KEY *for the* BABY BOY ACCESSORIES

THREADS & NEEDLES

DMC stranded cotton
A = 310 black
B = 321 vy lt garnet
C = 334 sky blue
D = 336 med navy blue

No. 9 straw (milliner's) needle

EMBROIDERY KEY

All embroidery is worked with two strands of thread unless otherwise specified.

Steam train

Driver's compartment = D
(8 bullion knots, 3 - 14 wraps)

Compartment roof = C
(2 bullion knots, 14 wraps)

Engine = B (12 bullion knots,
7 - 11 wraps)

Engine details = A (1 strand,
French knot, 1 wrap)

Chassis = C (5 bullion knots,
3 - 35 wraps, couching)

Engine front = C (4 bullion knots,
4 - 7 wraps)

Smoke stacks = A (5 bullion knots,
5 - 6 wraps)

Buffers = A (straight stitch)

Wheels = A (straight stitch,
French knot, 1 wrap)

Wheel outlines = A (1 strand,
back stitch)

Wheel links = A (1 strand,
straight stitch)

T H E
Blanket

by BEVERLEY GOGEL *of* NEW SOUTH WALES

When your little soul is tucked up snugly in the folds of this gorgeous

blanket you know he will very soon hear the magic music of sleep.

Sweet sleep, with soft down, Weave thy brows an infant crown! Sweet sleep, angel child.

WILLIAM BLAKE

The classic circular design is enhanced with sprays of bullion roses, rosebuds and daisies.

A border and lining of rich magnolia satin complements the ivory tones

of the embroidery and the pure wool doctor's flannel.

REQUIREMENTS

Fabric

94cm x 74cm wide (37" x 29 ⅛")
piece of ivory doctor's flannel

1.1m x 147cm wide (1yd 7 ¼" x 57 ⅞")
magnolia cathedral satin

Threads, Ribbons & Needles

See page 66.

Supplies

30cm (11 ¾") square of lightweight
non-fusible interfacing

Sharp HB lead pencil

PREPARATION FOR EMBROIDERY

See the centre liftout pattern for the
embroidery design.

Marking the design placement

Fold the piece of doctor's flannel into
quarters to find the centre. Mark the
centre point with a pin. Mark each
fold with pins for approximately
15cm (6") from the centre. Unfold
the fabric.

Transferring the design

Place the piece of interfacing over
the embroidery design in the centre
liftout pattern. Trace the design and
placement marks using a black pen.

Position the tracing onto the doctor's
flannel, aligning the placement
marks with the pins in the fabric.
Ensure the floral sprays on the edge
of the circle are oriented towards the
top and bottom of the blanket. Pin in
place to prevent movement.

Using the sharp lead pencil and
pressing firmly enough to pierce the
interfacing and mark the fabric,
mark dots at approximately 4mm
(³/₁₆") intervals around the entire
circle. Mark the centres of the roses
and curves of the sprays in the same
manner. Remove the tracing.

EMBROIDERY

See page 67 for step-by-step instructions
for grab stitch.

Use the straw needle for working the
bullion knots. The crewel needle is
used for the border and stems and
the chenille needle is used for the
petals, French knots and ribbon work.

The floral designs on each half of the
circle are embroidered in a similar
manner.

Order of Work

Circle

Using blended threads, embroider
the circle with stem stitch. Make each
stitch approximately 6mm (¼") long.
Pull the stitches firmly, however,
take care not to pucker the fabric.

Large peach sprays

Embroider the large peach bullion
rose first. Stitch two bullion knots
side by side for the centre. Surround
these with five overlapping bullion
knots for the petals.

Stitch the centres of the larger two
rosebuds with a single bullion knot
and work two bullion knots for the
outer petals. Embroider the petals
of the smaller rosebuds with two
bullion knots. Work two straight
stitches for the three smallest buds.

Embroider a grab stitch around each
bud to form the base of the calyx and
the stem. On some of the buds, work
one to two straight stitches along the
outer edges of the petals for the
remainder of the calyx.

"Play a little with the

straight stitch petals and buds.

Prod them softly from the front

with the eye of the needle to give

them body. Tug them gently at

the base from behind, again using

the eye of the needle. I always

strive for almond shaped petals

and buds and these techniques

help me to achieve this look."

BEVERLEY

The finished blanket measures 102cm x 82cm wide (40 ⅛" x 32 ¼")

Large pink sprays
Stitch the bullion rose and large and small bullion rosebuds in the same manner as the peach sprays. Work one single straight stitch bud with stranded cotton and the remaining straight stitch buds using the pink ribbon. Work the calyxes and stems as before.

Small peach and pink sprays
Work the bullion rose, rosebuds, calyxes and stems of each spray in the same manner as the large sprays.

Sprays of blue daisies
Add the sprays of blue daisies next. To add shading to each flower, the petals on one side are stitched in the lighter shade of thread and the others in the darker shade. Work the petals of the flowers and buds with two straight stitches prodding gently with the eye of the needle to give them shape.

Stitch the calyxes and stems in the same manner as the rosebuds, ensuring the anchoring stitches which form the stems link the flowers together. Add single straight stitches beside the flowers for leaves.

Sprays of ivory daisies
At the ends of the design, embroider the ivory sprays in a similar manner to the blue daisies. Use the pale gold ribbon for the flower petals within the circle. In each spray stitch one bud using two bullion knots. The remaining buds are stitched with one to two straight stitches.

Clusters of French knots
Scatter large blue and green French knots among the roses and add green knots to the daisies. Embroider two groups of three to four large pink French knots, positioning them near the pink rosebuds.

Foliage
Embroider pairs of tiny French knots near the tips of the daisies and add detached chain leaves.

CONSTRUCTION
See the centre liftout pattern.

THREADS, RIBBONS & NEEDLES

DMC stranded cotton

A = 225 ultra lt shell pink

B = 712 cream

C = 819 lt baby pink

D = 928 vy lt grey-green

E = 948 vy lt peach

F = 3013 lt khaki green

G = 3024 vy lt Jacobean green

H = 3072 vy lt beaver grey

Anchor stranded cotton

I = 387 stone

Madeira stranded cotton

J = 0306 vy lt peach

Waterlilies by Caron hand dyed
12 ply silk thread

K = 117 fresh pink

DMC no. 3 perlé cotton

L = 928 vy lt grey-green

YLI silk ribbon 4mm (³⁄₁₆") wide

M = 1.8m (1yd 34 ⅞") no. 5
pale pink

N = 90cm (35 ½") no. 34 pale gold

O = 1.8m (1yd 34 ⅞") no. 71
chartreuse

P = 90cm (35 ½") no. 73
antique blue

No. 1 straw (milliner's) needle

No. 7 crewel embroidery needle

No. 20 chenille needle

EMBROIDERY KEY

All thread embroidery is worked with
six strands unless otherwise specified.

Circle = F, G and H blended together
(1 strand of each, stem stitch)

Large peach spray

Rose

Inner petals = E (2 bullion knots,
11 wraps)

Outer petals = J (5 bullion knots,
15 wraps)

Large rosebuds

Inner petal = E (bullion knot,
11 wraps)

Outer petals = J (2 bullion knots,
9 - 10 wraps)

Small rosebuds

Petals = J (2 bullion knots, 6 - 9
wraps) or J (2 straight stitches)

Calyxes and stems = F, G and H
blended together (1 strand of each,
grab stitch, straight stitch)

Large pink spray

Rose

Inner petals = A
(2 bullion knots, 11 wraps)

Outer petals = C (5 bullion knots,
15 wraps)

Large rosebuds

Inner petal = A
(bullion knot, 11 wraps)

Outer petals = C (2 bullion knots,
9 - 10 wraps)

Small rosebuds

Petals = C (2 bullion knots, 6 - 9
wraps) or C (2 straight stitches)
or M (2 straight stitches)

Calyxes and stems = F, G and H
blended together (1 strand of each,
grab stitch, straight stitch)

Small peach spray

Rose

Inner petals = E
(3 strands, 2 bullion knots, 11 wraps)

Outer petals = J (3 strands, 5 bullion
knots, 15 wraps)

Rosebuds

Inner petal = E (3 strands,
bullion knot, 11 wraps) or none

Outer petals = J (3 strands, 2 bullion
knots, 10 wraps) or J (2 straight
stitches)

Calyxes and stems = F, G and H
blended together (1 strand of each,
grab stitch, straight stitch)

Small pink spray

Rose

Inner petals = A (3 strands, 2 bullion
knots, 11 wraps)

Outer petals = C (3 strands,
5 bullion knots, 15 wraps)

Rosebuds

Inner petal = A (3 strands, bullion
knot, 11 wraps) or none

Outer petals = C (3 strands,
2 bullion knots, 9 - 10 wraps)
or C (2 straight stitches)

Calyxes and stems = F, G and H
blended together (1 strand of each,
grab stitch, straight stitch)

Sprays of blue daisies

Petals = D and H (2 straight stitches)

Buds = D or H (2 straight stitches)

Calyxes and stems = F, G and H
blended together (1 strand of each,
grab stitch, straight stitch)

Sprays of ivory daisies

Petals = I and N (2 straight stitches)

Buds = B or N (2 straight stitches),
I (2 bullion knots, 10 wraps)

Calyxes and stems = F, G and H
blended together (1 strand of each,
grab stitch, straight stitch)

Clusters of French knots

French knots among roses = F, L,
O and P (French knot, 1 wrap)

French knots among daisies = F and O
(French knot, 1 wrap)

Pink French knots = K (3 - 6 strands,
French knot, 1 wrap)

Foliage

Small green French knots = F, G and H
blended together (1 strand of each,
French knot, 1 wrap)

Leaves = F, G and H blended
together (1 strand of each,
detached chain)

Bullion knot

Detached chain

French knot

Grab stitch

Stem stitch

Straight stitch

G R A B   S T I T C H

Grab stitch can be used to form the stems and calyx on buds and flowers. It needs to be worked in association with a stitch or stitches which you can slide a needle beneath.

For the step-by-step photographs we used three strands of stranded cotton.

1. Stitch the foundation stitch. Here we have used a bullion bud.

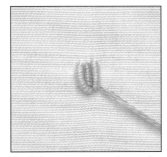

2. Bring the thread to the front just to the right hand side of the foundation stitch.

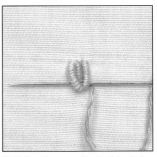

3. Take the needle behind the foundation stitch. Do not go through the fabric.

4. Pull the thread through, leaving a small loop on the right hand side.

5. Take the needle through the loop.

6. Pull the thread firmly. Take the needle to the back a short distance away and end off. **Completed grab stitch.**

THE First Dress

by ROBYN BEAVER *of* VICTORIA

IMPORTANT MILESTONES

First word, first tooth, first step, first dress.

And let it be a dress to rejoice in.

Of palest pink batiste with delicate ripples

of backsmocking and lashings of roses.

Greet the world little one.

The First Dress

When the first baby laughed for the first time, the laugh broke into a thousand pieces and they all went skipping about and that was the beginning of fairies.

from PETER PAN *by* J.M.BARRY

REQUIREMENTS
SIZES 3, 6 AND 12 MONTHS

Fabric & Lace

Pale pink Imperial batiste
112cm (44") wide

Size 3 months: 1.55m (1yd 25")

Size 6 months: 1.65m (1yd 29")

Size 12 months: 1.75m (1yd 33")

1m x 15mm wide (39 ½" x ⅝") white lace edging for all sizes

Threads & Needles

See page 72.

Supplies

2 x 11mm (⁷/₁₆") white pearl buttons

10cm (4") square lightweight fusible woven interfacing

Water-soluble fabric marker

PATTERN

See the centre liftout pattern.

The finished length from the centre back neckline to the hemline is

Size 3 months: 47cm (18 ½")

Size 6 months: 50cm (19 ¾")

Size 12 months: 53.5cm (21")

The hem allowance is 6cm (2 ⅜").

CUTTING OUT

See the centre liftout pattern for the cutting layout.

Pale pink Imperial batiste

Front: cut one,

Size 3 months: 58.5cm x 95cm wide (23" x 37 ⅜")

Size 6 months: 62.5cm x 102.5cm wide (24 ⅝" x 40 ⅜")

Size 12 months: 66.5cm x 110cm wide (26 ⅛" x 43 ⅜")

Trace the pattern pieces onto lightweight interfacing or tracing paper, transferring the pattern markings. Cut out all the pieces following the instructions in the centre liftout pattern.

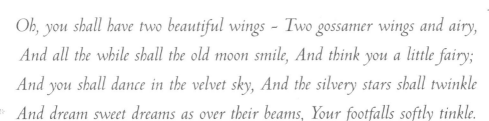

Oh, listen, little Dear-My-Soul, To the fairy voices calling,
For the moon is high in the misty sky, And the honey dew is falling;

Oh, you shall have two beautiful wings ~ Two gossamer wings and airy,
And all the while shall the old moon smile, And think you a little fairy;
And you shall dance in the velvet sky, And the silvery stars shall twinkle
And dream sweet dreams as over their beams, Your footfalls softly tinkle.

FAIRY AND CHILD *by* EUGENE FIELD

PREPARATION & PLEATING

See page 74 for step-by-step instructions for pleating.

Front

Pleat sixteen full space rows (including one lower holding row) with the top row 1cm (⅜") from the top raw edge. Unpick the pleating threads for 1cm (⅜") at each side for the seam allowance. Tie off the pleating threads to fit the front bodice lining pattern piece.

Sleeves

Cut a length of lace to fit the lower edge of each sleeve. With right sides together, pin the lace to the sleeve with the lace heading 2 - 3mm (⅛") from the raw edge. Using a narrow zigzag, roll and whip the lace to the lower edge of each sleeve. Press the seam towards the sleeve and the lace downwards.

Pleat five half space rows (including two holding rows) with the first row 2.5cm (1") from the seam. Unpick the pleating threads for 2cm (¾") at each side and tie off to measure approximately 16cm (6⅜").

SMOCKING

See page 75 for step-by-step instructions for trellis stitch.

All smocking is worked with the crewel needle.

Front bodice

Count the pleats and mark the centre valley.

Row 13 ½ - 14 ½. Begin at the centre two pleats on row 14 ½ with an under cable. Work six step trellis up to row 13 ½, over cable, three step trellis down to row 14, under cable, three step trellis up to row 13 ½, over cable, six step trellis down to row 14 ½. Continue the three step trellis - six step trellis combination to the end of the row. Turn the work upside down, return to the centre and complete the row.

Referring to the graph for thread colour placement, repeat the previous row three times, with the last row positioned between rows 14 - 15.

Backsmocking

The bodice is backsmocked with thirteen rows of two step trellis, beginning on row 1 - 1 ½ and ending on row 13 - 13 ½ . Refer to the graph for details.

Sleeves

On each sleeve, count the pleats and mark the centre valley.

Row 1 - 2. Begin at the centre two pleats on row 1 with an over cable. Work three step trellis down to row 2, under cable, three step trellis up to row 1.

Continue to the end of the row. Turn the work upside down, return to the centre and complete the row.

Referring to the graph for thread colour placement, repeat the previous row three times, with the last row worked between rows 2 - 3.

EMBROIDERY

All embroidery is worked with the straw needle.

Bodice embroidery

Following the graph for placement, work three bullion roses above each large 'V' shape and a single bullion rose above each small 'V' shape. For each rose, embroider two bullion knots side by side for the inner petals. Surround these with five bullion knots for the outer petals.

Following the graph for placement, stitch tiny green French knot buds and detached chain leaves around the roses.

Sleeve embroidery

Directly above each 'V' shape, work a single bullion rose in the same manner as those on the bodice. Add a detached chain leaf on both sides of each rose.

CONSTRUCTION

See the centre liftout pattern.

Embroidery Key For
THE FIRST DRESS

THREADS & NEEDLES

DMC stranded cotton
A = blanc
B = 503 med blue-green
C = 818 baby pink
D = 3688 med tea rose
E = 3689 lt tea rose

No. 8 crewel embroidery needle
No. 9 straw (milliner's) needle

SMOCKING & EMBROIDERY KEY

All embroidery is worked with two strands of thread unless otherwise specified.

Smocking

Smocking on bodice = A and E
(3 strands, 3 step trellis - 6 step trellis combination)

Backsmocking = C
(2 strands, 2 step trellis)

Smocking on sleeve = A and E
(3 strands, 3 step trellis)

Embroidery

Roses
Inner petals = D
(2 bullion knots, 6 wraps)

Outer petals = E
(5 bullion knots, 10 wraps)

Foliage
Leaves = B
(detached chain)

Buds = B (French knot, 1 wrap)

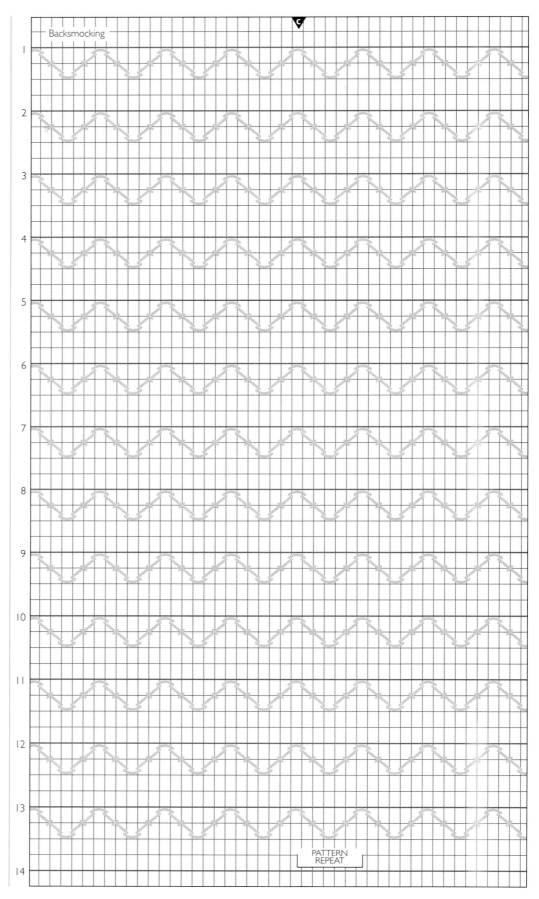

Front bodice

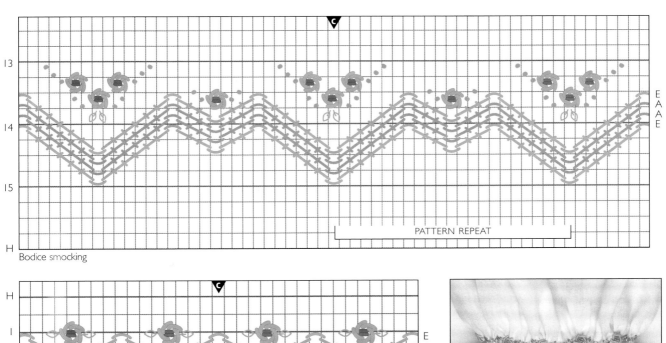

13

14

15

H

E
A
A
E

PATTERN REPEAT

Bodice smocking

H

1

2

3

H

E
A
A
E

PATTERN REPEAT

Sleeve (note: half space rows)

Sleeve

Smocking is worked on pre-pleated fabric. The quickest and easiest way to pleat the fabric is to use a pleating machine. If you do not have a pleater of your own, many needlework shops offer a pleating service. We used a Sally Stanley pleater which can pleat up to 24 full space rows or 15 half space rows.

PLEATING THE FRONT WITH FULL SPACE ROWS

1. Rolling up the fabric. With the wrong side uppermost, spread the fabric out flat. Ensure the top edge is to the right. With the end of the rod extending to the right, place it on the fabric.

2. Roll the fabric onto the rod, keeping it fairly firm but not tight. Place the rolled fabric through the left handle of the pleater behind the rollers.

3. Threading. Cut a long length of thread which contrasts with the fabric (dark colours may mark light coloured fabric). Beginning at the left, thread 16 needles with long thread. A needle threader makes this easier.

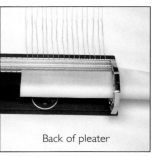

4. Pleating. Position the fabric into the groove at the back, ensuring the top edge is 1cm (⅜") beyond the last threaded needle.

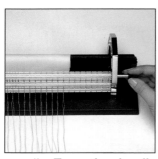

5. Turn the handle slowly away from you until you feel the fabric being gripped by the rollers.

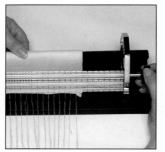

6. Continue turning the handle while guiding the fabric from behind. Ensure the top edge remains aligned.

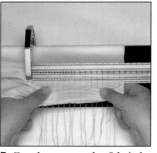

7. Gently remove the fabric by sliding it downwards and off the needles after every few turns.

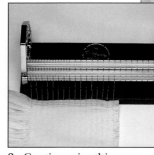

8. Continue in this manner until the entire piece of fabric is pleated. Completely remove the fabric and then the threads from the needles. **Completed pleated fabric.**

PLEATING THE SLEEVES WITH HALF SPACE ROWS

1. Preparation. Tilt the pleater backwards. Loosen end screws. Remove front roller. Reposition five needles each a half space apart on the left. Replace the roller and screws.

2. Roll one sleeve onto rod, keeping the lower edge on the right hand side. Place the rod behind the rollers. Thread the five needles with threads long enough for both sleeves.

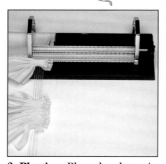

3. Pleating. Pleat the sleeve in the same manner as the front. Using the same threads, roll the second sleeve onto the rod and pleat.

4. When the threads are removed from the needles, separate the sleeves and cut the threads between them.

*Variations of trellis stitch are used to work the smocking on the sleeves,
front bodice and the backsmocking. Each variation is worked in the same manner.
For the step-by-step photographs we used three strands of stranded cotton.*

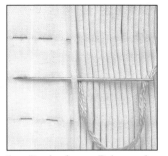

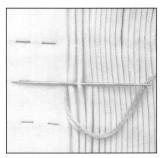

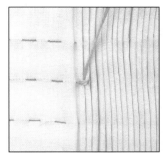

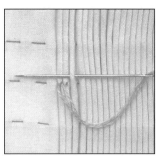

1. Beginning. Bring the thread to the front on a pleating row in the valley between the first two pleats. Take the needle from right to left through the first pleat ready to begin stitching.

2. Five step trellis. With the thread below the needle and keeping the needle horizontal, take it from right to left through the second pleat. Only pick up the top one third of the pleat.

3. Pull the thread through until the stitch rests gently against the pleats. **Completed under cable.**

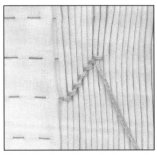

4. Stepping up. Step up one fifth of the way to the next pleating row. With the thread below the needle, take the needle from right to left through the next pleat.

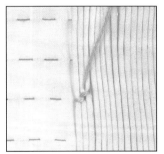

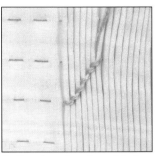

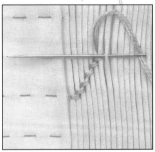

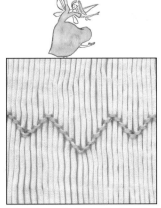

5. Pull the thread through.

6. Keeping the thread below the needle for each stitch, work four more stepped stitches the same distance apart, finishing on the pleating row above.

7. With the thread above the needle, take the needle from right to left through the next pleat, keeping it at the same level as the previous stitch.

8. Pull the thread through. This forms an over cable.

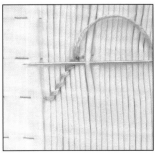

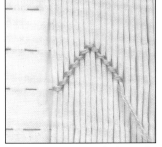

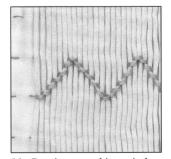

9. Stepping down. With the thread above the needle, take the needle from right to left through the next pleat one fifth of the way down to the pleating row below.

10. Pull the thread through. Work four more stepped stitches in the same manner, finishing on the pleating row below.

11. Continue working stitches in the same manner, using an over or under cable each time you change direction.

12. The stitches of the five step - three step trellis combination are worked in the same manner. Follow the graph for stitch placement.

T H E
Ball

by SUE GARDNER
of SOUTH AUSTRALIA

• LITTLE •

I am the sister of him, And he is my brother,

He is too little for us, To talk to each other.

So every morning I show him, My doll and my book;

But every morning he still is, Too little to look.

DOROTHY ALDIS

Love warms the cockles of your heart.

Love is making your baby a wonderous soft toy

decorated with creatures from the sea

and listening to a gentle tinkling from the bell enclosed within.

REQUIREMENTS

Fabric

*One piece of scarlet, orange,
mint green and aqua blue poplin each,
30cm x 25cm wide (11 ¾" x 9 ¾")*

Threads & Needles

See page 81.

Supplies

1m (39 ½") citron yellow mini piping

*30cm x 112cm wide (11 ¾" x 44")
lightweight fusible woven interfacing*

Polyester fibre-fill

*Cat's plastic ball with bell
approximately 5cm (2") wide*

15cm (6") embroidery hoop

Sharp lead pencil

Water-soluble fabric marker

PREPARATION FOR EMBROIDERY

*See the centre liftout pattern for the
embroidery designs.*

Preparing the fabric

Cut four pieces of interfacing, each
30cm x 25cm wide (11 ¾" x 9 ¾").
Fuse a piece of interfacing to the
wrong side of each piece of fabric.

Transferring the pattern

Trace the pattern piece onto lightweight interfacing or tracing paper,
transferring all pattern markings. Cut
out the pattern piece. Centre the
pattern piece onto the right side of
one piece of fabric. Trace around the
outline with the lead pencil. Repeat on
the three remaining pieces of fabric.

The fabric will be cut to the exact shape
after the embroidery is complete.

Transferring the embroidery designs

Using a black pen, trace each embroidery design onto a separate piece of
tracing paper.

Tape the goldfish design tracing to a
window or light box. Position the
aqua blue piece of fabric over the
tracing ensuring the design is centred
within the pattern outline. Tape in
place. The light shining through
will make the design lines easier to
see. Using the water-soluble fabric
marker, trace over all design lines.

Repeat the procedure for the
remaining three designs. Transfer the
angel fish design to the mint green
fabric, the school of fish design to the
orange fabric and the tortoise design
to the scarlet fabric.

EMBROIDERY

*See page 82 for step-by-step instructions
for raised stem stitch.*

Four colourful panels are embroidered to create a cheerful soft toy. The
aqua blue panel is embroidered with a
brightly coloured goldfish, stitched in
chain and stem stitch. The striking
angel fish, with embroidered black
and white stripes of chain stitch, is
worked on the mint green panel. A
school of four small striped fish,
stitched in stem stitch, swim among
the seaweed on the orange panel. The
scarlet panel is embroidered with a
tortoise, stitched mainly in chain and
raised stem stitch.

Use the no. 7 crewel needle for
stitching the grains of sand and the
tapestry needle for the raised stem
stitch. The no. 9 crewel needle is used
for all other embroidery. Place the
fabric in the hoop when working the
raised stem stitch, satin stitch, back
stitch and French knots.

The chain stitching
can be worked either
with the fabric in the
hoop or held freely
in the hand.

Order of work

Goldfish design

Stitch the side fin in raised stem stitch first. Using blended threads and beginning from the outer edges and working towards the centre, fill the body and tail with rows of chain stitch. Curve the rows to follow the shape of the body.

Leaving a space for the eye, embroider the head and remaining fins with rows of stem stitch worked closely together. Fill any remaining spaces with straight stitches. Cover the area for the eye with satin stitch. Add a French knot over the satin stitching for the pupil. Work all outlines in back stitch. Add straight stitches to the tail for markings.

Beginning at the base each time, stitch each piece of seaweed with two lines of stem stitch. The shorter piece of seaweed is partially worked over the fish. Using blended threads, add three French knots for the sand. Use one wrap for the upper knot and two wraps for the middle and lower knot.

Angel fish design

Embroider the body and tail with vertical lines of chain stitch. Turn the fabric upside down for each alternate row. Work the satin stitching for the eye over the chain stitching so it provides padding for the satin stitch. Embroider the two sections of the mouth in satin stitch.

Outline the mouth, eye, body and tail in back stitch. Extend the lines of back stitch out from the body and tail. Add a French knot to the centre of the eye.

Work the seaweed in the same manner as the previous design. Using blended threads, add six French knots near the base of the seaweed for the sand. Vary the number of wraps used to change the size of the grains.

School of fish design

Each fish is worked in the same manner. Embroider the orange-red body stripe with two rows of stem stitch which extend from the gills to the base of the tail. Beginning from the stripe and using the blue thread, fill the upper body and head with rows of stem stitch. Change thread colour and fill the lower body in the same manner. Stitch the upper fin and the two segments of the tail in satin stitch. For the lower fin, work straight stitches which all use the same hole in the fabric at the tip of the fin. Work the back stitch outlines and then stitch the mouth, eye, gill and upper fin markings over the previous embroidery.

Stitch the seaweed and sand in the same manner as before.

Tortoise design

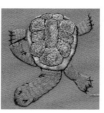

Stitch the plates of the shell first, completing one before beginning the next. Work each plate with rounds of chain stitch, working from the outer edge towards the middle. Outline the outer edge of the shell in split stitch. Ensuring the split stitch is completely covered, work satin stitch from the outer edge to the plates of the shell.

Embroider the head, neck and legs in raised stem stitch.

Work back stitch around each plate of the shell and partially outline the outer shell, legs, neck and head in the same manner. Embroider across the end of each foot in blanket stitch. Add straight stitches which extend out from the feet to complete the claws.

Stitch two small French knots for the nostrils and two uneven fly stitches for the eyes. Add straight stitches to the legs and neck to indicate creases in the skin.

Embroider the ripples of water in stem stitch. Finally, add a group of nine French knots at the lower edge of the design for sand in the same manner as the previous designs.

THESE DESIGNS USE

Back stitch, Blanket stitch, Split Stitch, Chain stitch, Fly stitch, French knot, Raised stem stitch, Satin stitch, Stem stitch, Straight stitch

THE *Ball*

THREADS & NEEDLES

DMC stranded cotton

A = *blanc*
B = *703 lt Kelly green*
C = *841 lt beige*
D = *996 med electric blue*
E = *3031 brown groundings*
F = *3047 lt yellow-beige*
G = *3371 black-brown*

Anchor stranded cotton

H = *332 bright tangerine*
I = *335 bright orange-red*

Minnamurra hand dyed stranded cotton

J = *200 brown sugar*

No. 7 crewel embroidery needle
No. 9 crewel embroidery needle
No. 24 tapestry needle

EMBROIDERY KEY

All embroidery is worked with two strands of thread unless otherwise specified.

Goldfish design

Fish

Side fin = H (raised stem stitch)

Body and tail = H blended with I (1 strand of each, chain stitch)

Head = H (1 strand, stem stitch, straight stitch)

Eye = F (1 strand, satin stitch), E (French knot, 4 wraps)

Upper and lower fins = H (1 strand, stem stitch)

Outlines = E (back stitch)

Tail markings = E (straight stitch)

Seaweed = B (1 strand, stem stitch)

Sand = 2 strands of F blended with 1 strand each of C and H (4 strands, French knot, 1 - 2 wraps)

Angel fish design

Fish

Body and tail = A and G (chain stitch)

Eye = F (satin stitch), G (French knot, 4 wraps)

Mouth = H (1 strand, satin stitch)

Outlines = G (back stitch)

Seaweed = B (1 strand, stem stitch)

Sand = 2 strands of F blended with 1 strand each of C and H (4 strands, French knot, 1 - 2 wraps)

School of fish design

Fish

Stripe = I (1 strand, stem stitch)

Upper body = D (1 strand, stem stitch)

Lower body = F (1 strand, stem stitch)

Upper fin = D (1 strand, satin stitch)

Upper fin markings = E (1 strand, straight stitch)

Tail = F (1 strand, satin stitch)

Lower fin = F (1 strand, straight stitch)

Eye = E (1 strand, French knot, 5 wraps)

Mouth = E (1 strand, straight stitch)

Gill markings = E (1 strand, back stitch)

Outlines and body markings = E (1 strand, back stitch)

Seaweed = B (1 strand, stem stitch)

Sand = 2 strands of F blended with 1 strand each of C and H (4 strands, French knot, 1 - 2 wraps)

Tortoise design

Tortoise

Shell = J (chain stitch; 1 strand, split stitch, satin stitch)

Head and neck = C (raised stem stitch)

Legs = C (raised stem stitch)

Outlines = E (1 strand, back stitch)

Claws = E (1 strand, blanket stitch, straight stitch)

Nostrils = E (French knot, 2 wraps)

Eyes = E (fly stitch)

Markings = E (1 strand, straight stitch)

Water = D (1 strand, stem stitch)

Sand = 2 strands of F blended with 1 strand each of C and H (4 strands, French knot, 1 - 2 wraps)

CONSTRUCTION

See the centre liftout pattern.

Raised stem stitch is created from a foundation of straight stitches upon which rows of stem stitch are embroidered. It is best to work this stitch in a hoop, using a crewel needle for the foundation stitches and a tapestry needle for the stem stitch.

For the step-by-step photographs we used two strands of stranded cotton and contrasting threads.

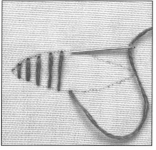

1. Foundation. Work parallel straight stitches at right angles to the outline keeping them approx. 3mm (1/8") apart. Start and finish the stitches exactly on the marked outline.

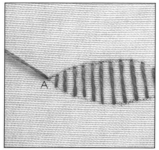

2. Raised stem stitch. Using a new thread, bring the needle to the front at A, on the left hand side of the shape.

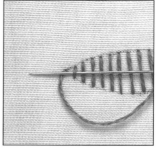

3. Pull the thread through. Keeping the thread below the needle, take the needle from right to left under the first straight stitch. The needle does not go through the fabric.

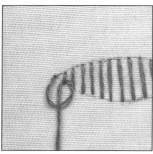

4. Begin to gently pull the thread downwards.

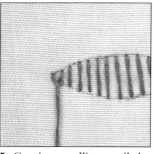

5. Continue pulling until the stem stitch wraps firmly around the straight stitch. **Completed first raised stem stitch.**

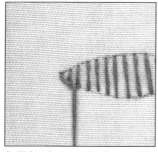

6. Take the needle from right to left under the next straight stitch. Holding it in place, pull the thread through in the same manner as the first stitch.

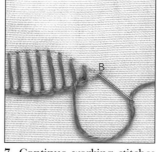

7. Continue working stitches to the end of the shape. Slide the needle behind the straight stitches and pack the stem stitches down. Take the needle to the back at B, at the end of the shape.

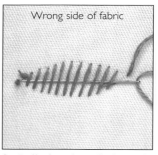

8. Pull the thread through. Turn the fabric to the wrong side. Slide the needle under the straight stitches on the back of the fabric.

9. Turn the fabric to the right side. Re-emerge just above A. Work a second row of raised stem stitch in the same manner as the first. The rows of stitches will touch each other.

10. Continue working rows in the same manner, packing each row down. As the shape fills, start and finish rows away from the tips of the shape so they don't become too thick and bulky.

11. Continue working rows of stem stitch until the shape is filled and the straight stitches are completely covered. Take the thread to the back exactly on the marked outline.

12. Pull the thread through and end off on the back. **Completed raised stem stitch.**

Heartfelt thanks to the many talented people who have made this book possible

THE CONTRIBUTORS *Alla Akselrod, Robyn Beaver, Jenny Brown, Gabrielle Francis, Sue Gardner, Beverley Gogel, Kris Richards, Jenny Saladine and Sharon Venhoek*

THE EDITORIAL AND DESIGN TEAM *Kathleen Barac, Margie Bauer, Chris Brazier, Gabrielle Canny, Marian Carpenter, Helen Davies, Sue Gardner, Lizzie Kulinski, Lahn Stafford Design, Coral Moss and Susan O'Connor*

A very special thank you to Coral Moss, who was so instrumental in bringing this publication to fruition.

PHOTOGRAPHY *Andrew Dunbar*

PHOTOGRAPHIC ASSISTANT *Jennie Groom*

STYLIST *Shyla Bauer*

FILM SEPARATIONS *van Gastel Graphics*

PRINTING *van Gastel Printing*

PUBLISHER *Country Bumpkin Publications*

Proudly produced and printed in South Australia

COUNTRY BUMPKIN
PUBLICATIONS

Country Bumpkin Publications
PO Box 194, Kent Town, South Australia, 5071, Australia
76A Kensington Road, Rose Park, South Australia, 5067, Australia
Telephone: (08) 8364 1075, int 61 8 8364 1075
Facsimile: (08) 8364 0479, int 61 8 8364 0479
Email: cbumpkin@ozemail.com.au

INSPIRATIONS BABY
ISBN 0 9577159 19